FILM

&

VIDEO

FINANCING

by

Michael Wiese

i

Published by Michael Wiese Productions, 3960 Laurel Canyon
Boulevard, Suite #331, Studio City, CA 91604, (818) 905-6367 in
conjunction with Focal Press, a division of Butterworth Publishers, 80
Montvale Avenue, Stoneham, MA 02180, (617) 438-8464.

Cover design by Barry Grimes, Los Angeles
Front & back cover photographs by Geraldine Overton

Printed by Braun-Brumfield, Inc., Ann Arbor, Michigan.
Manufactured in the United States of America.

Copyright 1991 by Michael Wiese
First Printing July 1991

Note: The information presented in this book is for educational
purposes only. The author is not giving business or financial advice.
Readers should consult their lawyers and financial advisors on their
business plans and procedures. The publisher is not liable for how
readers may choose to use this information.

The publisher plants two trees for every tree used in the
manufacturing of this book. Printed on recycled stock.

ISBN 0-941188-11-6

Books by MICHAEL WIESE

Film & Video Financing
Film & Video Marketing
Home Video: Producing for the Home Market
Film & Video Budgets
The Independent Film & Videomaker's Guide

Audiotape by MICHAEL WIESE

The American Film Institute Seminar: Financing & Producing Video

Books from MICHAEL WIESE PRODUCTIONS

Film Directing Shot by Shot by Steven D. Katz
Hollywood Gift Catalog by Ernie Fosselius
Fade In: The Screenwriting Process by Robert A. Berman

88993

FOR GERALDINE OVERTON

On the eve of our marriage.

CONTENTS

ACKNOWLEDGEMENTS

"This is my fifth book. It can't take that long to write," I said to myself. And off I went typing. Now, nearly three years later, it's finally complete. There are many people who have helped, pulled, tugged and nurtured my writing process that deserve acknowledgement.

I started the book not long before I met my wife, Geraldine Overton. Writing a finance book is not what one wants to be doing when romance and enchantment are in full bloom, but nevertheless I kept on typing. Fortunately, Geraldine—a stylish photographer and collector of rare first editions—loves books. So whenever I had to write, during a weekend or before dawn or after midnight, she was wonderfully supportive—tea and snacks were never scarce. She has guided me to new authors, ideas, art, and music. We travelled to exotic and faraway lands. She took the terrific photograph of the author on the back cover.

The process of gathering the knowledge and experience found in this book comes through my associations with many, many people. Sometimes they concurred on how things are done, sometimes not. This book, like a snapshot in time, is a reflection of how financing happens today. Hopefully the principles embodied here will be applicable tomorrow. My thanks go out to everyone I talked to in the course of writing the book, whether I quoted them or not: Greg Johnson, Rob Straight, Larry Kasanoff, Sam Grogg, Robert Rautenberg, Bobby Newmeyer, Richard Lorber, Stephen Cunningham, Harold Messing, and Steve Monas.

During the course of writing this book, I've had the opportunity to learn as well from those companies and individuals who've employed me as writer, consultant or producer. These people have also contributed to the experiential well from which I drew during the writing of this book. They include Michael Nesmith, Al Cattabiani, George Steele and Joanne Held of Pacific Arts/PBS Home Video; David Crippens, Tim Conroy, Dick Cook and Gary Ferrell of KCET Television/Lifeguides Video; Emily Laskin, James Hindman and Nick DeMartino of The American Film Institute and The AFI/Apple Media Lab, Brian McKernan, editor of *Videography*, production partner Steve Michelson and consulting partner Janice Whiffen.

Barry Grimes of Barry Grimes Design, Los Angeles not only designed the cover for this book and the newly published *Film Directing Shot By Shot* by Steven Katz, but he also designed video packages, book flyers, and opening titles, as well as souped up my computer for me. He's the best.

Karen Speerstra, senior editor at Focal Press and treasured friend, has been through a number of books (and one audiotape) with me now. We laugh, we cry, we miss deadlines. My thanks go out to her for joining the rollercoaster ride and for still hanging on.

"Hi, this is Mary," is a voice I hear several times a week which belongs to Mary Murrell, my account representative at Braun-Brumfield, the printing company. From the very first book, Mary's frequent calls come in response to handling the myriad details that come with printing, inventory, and shipping. Dick Bunnell of New England Book Components is responsible for shepherding the printing of the color covers. Both these people are top-notch professionals and regardless of offers to me from their competing printers, it's people like Mary and Dick that keep me where I am.

Janis Ringel of The Word Expressed did the copyediting and proofing of the text and layout. Without her left-brained meticulousness, I'm sure I'd be incomprehensible. Her consistency is a rare skill indeed. I don't even write my own name the same way twice!

Lastly, and perhaps most importantly, you and other readers, who have bought and used my last four books, attended my seminars, involved me in your projects and frequently let me know that my work has made a contribution to you in helping your projects get financed, produced, distributed and marketed. Without you there would be no books and no one with whom to share this information. I hope this book, too,contributes to the success of your work.

Michael Wiese
Studio City, CA
May 13, 1991

INTRODUCTION

INTRODUCTION

"We believe in you—now go do it."

Introduction

The toughest thing is getting the money. Money seems to be scarce. Movie ideas are plentiful. Everybody's got a script. Getting the money is what makes the difference. And it is even tougher when you learn that there is really no road map about how to go about it. Why should others share their money-raising ideas with you, especially if they already feel there isn't enough money to go around?

Financing is that mysterious, illusive undertaking in which only those with boundless energy set off and return. And how wonderful it is to find support and backing for your projects—regardless of whether it comes from friends, from investors, from distributors, from foreign buyers or from grant-giving foundations. Somebody said *"yes."* Someone said, *"We believe in you—now go do it."*

This book is an attempt at sorting out the different options that producers have in financing their film and video projects. It will also be of use to television producers and creators of other forms of media. In fact, the dividing lines among media are blurring. A single communication piece may end up in any of a variety of markets: theatrical, home video, pay per view, pay television, and syndication, both foreign and domestic. And each producer's "palette" may be filled with a variety of "colors" and strategies for raising the financing.

There are some basic strategies that many agree are the way to go, but for every so-called "traditional" financing deal there are 10 other arrangements that were put together in creative and ingenious ways. Therefore, the role of the producer is to assess his or her skills and resources and come up with a strategy that will raise the money in the shortest time.

My advice is primarily intended for independent producers of independent features and for home video producers. The budgets we'll discuss are generally lower than studio films, although there is nothing to keep ambitious producers from using the strategies in this book for packaging more expensive productions. In fact, the strategies in this book are for independent producers going the "non-studio" route.

Publication of this book probably couldn't come at a better time since—thanks to the video boom—more and more feature film producers have entered the playing field. But it also probably couldn't have come at a worse time because the competition—not only among independents but among the vertically integrated major corporate players (who own the studios)—has greater control of all channels of distribution. The screens and distribution paths not controlled by the majors that are available to independent distributors throw off less than 5 percent of the total motion picture domestic revenues. It's a very tough world out there. It's my sincere hope that the information contained in this book makes it a little easier.

Most filmmakers don't think financing is very creative. They'd rather not know about it, nor do it, until they finally wake to the notion that without financing their dreams would never be manifest, their ideas would stay unshared, and their stories would never be told. While financing is not something we usually look forward to doing, it is what gets the production wheels turning.

The thrust of this book is that financing is creative. Very creative. This book is, therefore, a kind of pallet for producers. But it's the producer, not this author, who must paint his picture using whatever resources he or she can muster. This book isn't the end all to financing but rather, a beginning. My pallet of financing options, suggestions, and ideas will enable you to develop your own techniques, approaches, and procedures to finance your films and videos.

To keep from becoming overwhelmed, you must assess your own abilities and resources and then clearly determine a strategy. This will involve prioritizing your resources, clarifying your intent, preparing a prospectus, drawing up a business plan, and so forth, and then setting out on the financing journey. So this book may also serve as an idea generator to prepare you for your financing sortie. When you find that what you are doing isn't getting the job done (e.g., raising money) you must take that as a cue to try something else. You may find that you can return to this book to embellish your initial ideas and make them more useful. Go through the questions in the "Questions" section of the book. This is a valuable process, one that bears fruit with every use. It unlocks the ideas and resources you already have but may have forgotten.

Your role as reader is to "go to school" on the ideas in the book. (Fold down pages, yellow favorite lines, and write down your ideas as you get them and as they pertain to your own projects.) Then go to school on your peers and the industry leaders who've come up with this year's financing models. Let them inspire you to find new twists on how to obtain financing and the other resources you need. There is no one way. There are many ways. Whether you want to or not, you'll probably be blazing a new trail. Now start reading—you've got money to raise!

FILM
PRODUCTION
OVERVIEW

FILM PRODUCTION OVERVIEW

"In a few years there will be a need for more product.
The question is, who will supply it?"

Overview

It may behoove us to explore the fire before jumping from the frying pan and get a overview of the time-consuming journey called "financing your film." What has been happening recently in motion picture production?

Independent production is in a declining cycle, and this is not good news for independent producers. Because less money is being made by independent films in the marketplace, in the last ten years it has been more difficult than ever for independents to raise money. The problem is that there is no real way to fractionalize rights anymore. The old game was that the parts were greater than the whole. This isn't true today because distributors want all-rights deals, and the prices offered may not cover the cost of production. In the old days, a producer could be into profit before the film went into production by selling off rights in a film piece by piece.

This does not mean that a particular film cannot perform well. It just means you have to be smarter and better prepared than your competitors, who are also trying to raise money. The rule of thumb in motion picture financing today says that you look to foreign sources to cover from 40 to 50 percent of your budget. As for box office receipts, a film has to earn more because the dollar has fallen in strength.

In 1988 the studios financed from 100 to 110 movies and released 157. The films they didn't produce they "picked up." The total number of all films produced was about 500. In 1989 the total number declined to 400, a 20 percent drop in production. The greatest decline was among independent producers.

In 1985 the average studio film cost about $17 million. Today the average studio film costs $24 million. In 1985 the average print and ad cost for a film was about $6.5 million. Today the cost exceeds $10 million a film, and 22 percent of the gross theatrical rentals is spent on marketing. The studios spend this much to "buy grosses" and to increase their overall market share. At this spending level they are able to keep theatrical tracks (the best theaters) while keeping other studio pictures and independent pictures away from the best screens. This is very big business. Stars in these movies receive from $2 to $7 million, directors get from $1 to $3 million, and writers collect as much as $3 million for a screenplay. It's a very rarified strata. With these elements and expenditures it comes as no surprise that theatrical exhibitors choose these films over independent products.

These bigger films are grossing a bigger share of the revenues. In 1985 there were 13 films that grossed over $20 million; in 1986, 17; in 1987, 20; in 1988, 18; and in 1989, 30.

Since 1985 the box office grosses have grown from $3.7 billion to over $5 billion. The majors receive 95 percent or more of all theatrical grosses. (However, from 15 to 20 percent of the films they release are independently financed and picked up later by the studios.)

Back on earth, independents make films in the $6- to $7-million range, with from $3 to $5 million allotted for prints and advertising. Many will argue that you cannot release a film nationally on $2 to $5 million because, they say, the P&A (print and advertising) budget is what's necessary to boost home video sales and the other ancillary values. However, this is what a mini-major generally spends on launching a film. Most agree that the days are over when you could do a token theatrical release to con the home video industry into thinking your picture had undergone the genuine article. Even limited exposure requires a release in from 10 to 15 markets. (An exception to this is a film that has an actor (Gene Hackman, Mickey Rourke, Michael Caine) with a strong home video following that will rent anything the star is in.)

The film business is cyclical and there are often highs and lows. The last few years have been a low period for independents. Fewer films are being made in the under-$8-million budget range. Once independents were making up to 80 percent of the total number of pictures in the $8-million range; now they are making about 50 percent. Once the total market share for independents was 5 percent; now it has fallen from 2 to 3 percent.

The consolidation and creation of huge companies, which control a greater and greater percentage of the market, are driving alternative distributors—particularly the mid-sized companies—out of business. This is because alternative distributors have 1) an overhead too high to survive on very low- budget or art pictures where the upside isn't substantial, and 2) little available capital. The mid-size companies just can't compete on a financial basis with the majors and they self-destruct. In the last few years, many of the small and mid-sized independent film companies making $8-million films went belly up. Companies like Skouras, MCEG, Miramax, Cinecom, New World, New Line and a few others have been able to hang on, and a few are showing some strength.

Serious, adult movies were once the domain of independent producers. The studios were off doing teen genre films. When audiences began growing up and wanted to see more sophisticated fare, the majors entered the adult field and released such pictures as DANGEROUS LIAISONS, HOPE AND GLORY, DEAD

11

RINGER, DO THE RIGHT THING, MOONSTRUCK, and
WHEN HARRY MET SALLY and distributed them more widely. All
had name talent. Only a few years ago the studios wouldn't have given
a wide release to these pictures. This has increased pressure on the
independents who find it difficult to compete with the majors in an
adult genre that they once had to themselves.

Wall Street became disenchanted with filmmaking, having seen many
film companies go bankrupt with public funds and too many investors
lose out. Most deals didn't work. One exception was Silver Screen, a
highly visible and successful motion picture offering, which was more
like a loan finance deal than an investment. The partners got a 14 to
18 percent guaranteed return on their money and very small
participation. But it earned a strong return for investors. And it was
not a tax-driven deal, which in the U.S. are virtually dead.

That's the bad news. The good news is that there are new
opportunities for independently produced films, particularly in
Europe, that include satellite and pay television. The emergence of
high-definition television and interactive video is only a few years
away. Markets are opening in Eastern Europe, the Soviet Union, and
China. The total revenues from sales at The American Film Market
for television, theatrical and home video combined continue to rise in
Europe and the Far East with revenues of $744 million and $236
million respectively in 1990. U.S. film exports in 1989 were $1.7
billion; in 1990 it grew to $1.9 billion. Ninety-four percent of
industry leaders feel that U.S. films will continue to dominate
international trade by the year 2000.

VCRs are now in over 65 million homes or more than 70 percent of
U.S. TV households. From 1988 to 1989 sales of pre-recorded videos
to dealers increased nearly 50 percent. People are buying and
collecting videos.

Video rental stores are stocking depth rather than breadth. This means that they will stock a lot more "A" titles and risk having too few titles of all films. The good news for independents is that films previously called "small" or "art" or "adult" films like the MOONSTRUCKs or WHEN HARRY MET SALLYs are now becoming "A's." Previously these "small movies" with small independent distributor-type releases (50 to 200 prints) sold from 5,000 to 50,000 video units. They are now selling from 150,000 to 200,000 units.

In terms of household viewing, the average television set is on 49 hours a week or more than 7 hours each day.

Television and cable continues to be a good market although in-house production has increased. USA Network airs 24 films a year. Showtime, Lifetime, Viacom, and HBO all have film production arms. Turner's TBS and TNT movie channels are doing original films. Showtime, for example, makes films for from $3 to $4 million. They will totally finance a film and keep all rights. If half of 5 million homes see it, every TV critic will review it, and a film will get exposure even without a theatrical showing.

There is an increase in the number of theatrical screens being built here and abroad. The circuits are growing and that will create renewed opportunities. In the U.S. there were 18,000 screens in 1985. By the end of 1989 there were 22,000 screens. In a few years there will be a need for more product. The question is, who will supply it? The studios can only produce from 125 to 150 pictures each year as their upper limit, whereas from 300 to 400 films are needed to fill more than 25,000 theaters. Exhibitors will always look at independent films just because there are so many screens to fill. To get a booking and any real attention, independents will need to impress the exhibitor with good ideas.

13

Clearly, programming will continue to be in demand.

That's where you come in. Before we examine specific ways to raise the money, let's see what attitude carries a producer to successful financing.

ATTITUDE

AND

APPROACH

ATTITUDE AND APPROACH

"No one wants to be first, no one wants to be left out."

Attitude and Approach

Believe it or not but your script, prospectus, and income projections are only a small part of what it takes to get financing. The key ingredient is you and your creative team. As much as you may wish to shift the attention from yourself and onto your script or business plan, the investors will be looking to you to get the job done. Everything will rest on you. So it's time to start wearing an air of responsibility and competency and assume other characteristics that elicit backing and confidence.

Investors are investing in you. They will be drawn into a project by you. You think it's a good idea. They think it's a good idea. They want to believe in what you tell them. If you are enthusiastic (and realistic) about making your film, they'll believe you can do it. Even before you go to investors you must be completely confident in your own abilities and what you are doing. You must be more confident than you've ever been before, because that's what it will take. If you have this kind of clear focus, intensity and commitment about making your film, nothing will stop you. You will find your financing for one reason—because you simply won't stop until you get it. That kind of certainty is infectious, and very tangible to investors. That's what they're investing in. They are investing in you.

Attitude

Therefore your attitude is very simple. You have a great determination to get your film or video produced. At the same time, this doesn't mean you are inflexible or unwilling to listen, nor do you

17

appear overbearing or conceited. To gain support all along the way, you must be open and always moving forward, conveying the impression that regardless of whether people join you or not, you will reach your end goal. If you communicate that, you will get what you need.

Commitment is perhaps the most important quality to possess because it will carry you further. And this you will need because producing is a very long process. With commitment you can go about seeking advice, support and financing from others.

Healthy enthusiasm and spirit are qualities that attract others. You can't go overboard here. I've met many producers who were enthusiastic and can go on and on about how great their project is. But somehow I had the feeling they were never going to get their film made. Why? Because they weren't able to listen, or to be realistic, or to study the marketplace, or be grounded in reality, or really allowed others to help them. They were defensive, inflexible, in too much of a hurry, and wanted to do it their own way.

I know what this is like because I've been there. I was once in too much of a hurry to get a film that I'd finished into the hands of a distributor. Along the way I met an experienced executive producer and producer's rep in the movie business. He liked me, he liked my film, and he said he'd help, not only in placing this film but in getting the next one going. But in my impatient eyes he moved too slowly. He was not setting up screenings or sending me to meetings. I thought he was an agent. So I, anxious to get going, set up my own meetings and found my own distributor. What I failed to realize is that his contacts, used slowly, may have yielded better results than my own. He thought long term. I wanted it done now. His experience could have saved weeks or months or years of running around. But I didn't respect that. I was too independent to let someone help. I'll never know what I lost by not allowing a more experienced producer to take me under his wing.

This is a common occurrence. Sometimes by flailing around you overlook opportunities. Producers can benefit by carefully thinking about and designing their strategy, rather than going off half-cocked. Investors and distributors can sense the difference.

Think about Kevin Costner or Michael Douglas or Jane Fonda for a minute. Whether what I am about to say is true or not I don't know (because I've never met these folks) but I suspect it is. They naturally exude the kind of confidence that I'm talking about. They are clearly committed, intelligent people, and you can bet that when they set out to do something, people are there to say "okay." And I'm not talking about the fact that they are movie stars but rather about the kind of energy they radiate. That's the kind of energy you need to have for your project. And it needs to be visible to others. Those around you also need to bring this kind of focus and attention to your project. This commitment, including those from investors, is what gets your project made.

Experience

Then there's the track record. Investors want to see what else you've done that was successful (or at least impressive). If you don't have much of a track record, then find partners who do, who can bring the "get it done" experience to the overall package. This is a must. Investors are skittish enough as it is and will be frightened off by lack of experience. Remember that a film or video project is a small business. If the majority of small businesses in this country fail because of lack of experience, many films and videos are destined to the same fate.

Strong Package

You've got the right attitude and energy, you've got the experience, so are you there yet? Now you need a great script, a fine cast, and other creative partners that elevate your project above all the others. Your package must also be designed so that when it comes time to market the film, there will be many promotable elements. Distributors must clearly see how to sell your film or video.

Resources and Network

With all of this in line, you must now rally all your resources, your friends' resources, and your friends' friends' resources to get your film or video financed and made. If you are at all shy about calling on your friends, not to mention people you don't even know, then you won't have what it takes to get your film made. Better find a partner who can do this.

If you don't have the willingness to put yourself out again and again, and suffer frequent rejection, you should not be in this business. Those who succeed are those who talk all day and work at it until it gets done. They seem to thrive on adversity. A rejection doesn't send them into a depression but stimulates their desire to succeed. A very healthy exercise for all producers would be to spend some time assessing their true feelings and willingness to pitch their projects. Do they have the energy for it? More important, are they really fully committed deep down? Probably not as much as they need to be. If they were more projects would get made.

It took me a very long time to realize something about commitment. When a project came along I always felt I had to direct it. I only had one way to relate to a project: If I couldn't direct it, I didn't want to do it. Over the years I realize that, with projects, like people, you can choose the kind of relationship you wish to have. With projects you can make this determination at the outset. It's a very important thing to do. It does not behoove you to rush into a project without considering your level of commitment. If you know your relationship to the project, you can determine your level of commitment. And since investors, for one, will be looking to you (and your partners), it's important that you know exactly where you stand.

To give an example, I always thought that what I wanted to do was direct. That meant that I wanted to direct every project that came along. It didn't matter whose project it was or where it came from, I wanted to direct. Now that didn't leave a whole lot of room for anything else because directing requires complete, absolute, total commitment. That meant that on every project that I was to direct, I had to have complete, absolute, total commitment. When you are directing you can't do anything else. You are totally focused on one project and the details of that project. Your mind is filled with how to improve what you are doing. Directing can take a long time. When you direct, there are other projects you are choosing not to do. That meant, I didn't give myself the option to do anything else at the same time. Every project was to be totally consuming. Finally a light bulb went off in my head. I realized that if I asked myself the truth about all these projects, I wasn't absolutely, totally, myopically, committed to just directing. In fact, like friends, there is a whole world of other relationships I could have. I had been looking at the world of filmmaking in a very narrow way.

I began to think of my relationships to projects in a different way. Think of a series of concentric circles: a kind of a like target pattern. The bull's eye or inner most circle is directing. It's small in relationship to the other circles. That means that—because of the totality of directing—that if I chose to direct, there will be few instances of directing in a particular period of time. And that has turned out to be true. Once every 2 years there may be a project that I care enough about, that really grabs me, and engages me enough that I'll want give up everything else just to direct it. I've found I've got to be very committed to muster the energy to pull it off. I have to know within myself that there is enough depth in the project for me to want to be obsessed by it for a long time. Directing is reserved for the projects I care very, very much about on a deeply personal level. And so the directing circle is small and there are few things I direct.

That's true. Now I don't even think about directing every project even though at this stage of my career there are a good number of directing opportunities. Generally I produce.

The next circle is larger and can hold a few more projects a year. This is producing. Producing isn't as consuming for me as directing. Every year there may be one or two or three projects that I can and will produce. These are projects that I care about and want to have a hand in making.

The next concentric circle out is executive producing. At this level I can work on many more projects a year (five or six or seven or more). Executive producing is producing producers. These are projects that I choose to oversee and nurture at every stage. My time isn't required on every single task; I don't get involved in the minutiae; I may not go to every shoot or approve every invoice or look at all the dailies.

The outermost circle is consulting. These projects usually come to me. Sometimes people may want me to direct, or produce, or executive produce, but for various reasons I don't. I may want to help but not have the time, or I may feel that my time is not best used in that manner. So I consult. This is the largest circle and I can do a lot of consulting on a lot of projects every year. In a few hours or a few days or a few weeks I may be able to contribute, influence, and touch these projects in just the right way and at the right time. In many instances, and particularly with out-of-town clients, I may not even see the film or video until it has been completed.

I am still committed but my level of commitment is commensurate with the job. I don't have to fool myself or anyone else because I am exactly where I want to be. Overall, it gives me much more freedom of choice in determining the level at which I relate to my projects.

Integrity

The point of this exercise is to discover your true relationship to the project. In your most private moment is this project what you should really be doing right now? What should you really do? How much do you really care about this project? Does it have enough depth for you to be able to work on it passionately every day? For years? Or will you run out of steam in six months? If your interest is depleted, who will bring it across the finish line? You have to determine your level of commitment to a project and stand by your decision, especially if you are about to line up investors and ask for their commitment, their cash. If you tell yourself the truth, then everyone you come into contact with (including investors) will feel your level of commitment and feel a lot better about working with you.

What we're really talking about here is integrity: that intangible thing that investors will sense within moments of meeting you. Do I believe this producer who is asking for my money? Will he or she get the job done? Will the film or video be as good later as he or she says it will? Is the producer knowledgeable and experienced enough to shepherd the project all the way through production and distribution? Is the producer savvy enough to know an unfair distribution deal? Will the producer be able to collect the money when the film or video earns it? Am I aligned with the producer's values? And a thousand other questions...

This all comes back to the producer. To you. To your commitment to the project and to your integrity, which is really where the investment is being made.

Personal Power

The beginning is the most difficult. You will have to have significant personal power to avoid the chicken-and-egg problem inherent in production. Which is: No one wants to be first. No one wants to be the first to invest, or to be in a film, or to direct it, or even to write it.

The secret is to build up confidence and agreement around yourself and your project. How do you do that? How do you get your confidence up when no one has signed up? Personal power. Your own devotion to the project must be so strong that the "I don't want to be first" feeling is broken. Your devotion also has to be balanced. (There are many producers running around out there with very unrealistic expectations about their projects and how to do things. It's clear upon meeting them that they are inexperienced and their heads are in the clouds. This is not the kind of devotion I am talking about.) It's a matter of perception, how you and your project are perceived. Start slowly.   Build critical mass. Begin gathering those elements that will bring the greatest credibility first. The script, the actors, the director. *If I can raise the money by August will you appear in it? If you like the script and if I get so-and-so to be in it will you invest? If "yes," will you give me a letter of interest?*

Once you've done this a few times you are on your way to building agreement around your project. *(We all agree this is a good idea and we support it.)*   Others will begin to be attracted to the power and commitment and agreement you are beginning to receive. **No one wants to be first, but no one wants to be left out.**

This is all accomplished through your attitude and commitment. When you've amassed agreement among the major players (writer, director, actors) and they are pretty much at the same place, it's time to close the deal. With all the pieces in place you move everyone from "interest" to "intent" and begin getting contracts signed. To get each person to move forward is a direct reflection of your personal power, and your own knowledge of your assessment of their level of commitment. (If they are not really committed then your package starts to fall apart. You have to tell yourself the truth about their real level of interest or commitment to your project.) Eventually it becomes collective power. Then you're really moving.

ATTITUDE AND APPROACH

RESOURCES

RESOURCES

"Investors and buyers want you to have done all the work for them before making a decision."

Resources

What resources do I need to begin? Before a frontal assault on the world of investors, banks, and deal-making, the producer needs to have an arsenal of information, contacts, and elements for his or her production already in place. **The more developed and complete the package the greater the opportunity for financing.** Investors and buyers want all the work done for them, all the information in front of them, in order to make a decision. The producer's job is to provide this information. Assembling all the pieces can take months, or more likely, years, to put in place. In this chapter we'll review the main elements that make up your project (like the budget) or stand behind your project (like your lawyer or accountant). Terms or concepts that you may not fully understand will be explained in later chapters.

Development Ability—"Packaging"

A producer first must ascertain whether he has the talent and abilities to develop properties and put projects together. Not everyone has the skills, sensitivity, and ability to sniff out good properties and people. Working for years to put together a production that is unattractive to a buyer, a distributor, and an audience is a paramount waste of time. In the short run, it may be ego-gratifying to call yourself a producer and run around "producing a movie," but unless it eventually gets made you will never feel very good about your "years in the movie

29

business." If you don't have the qualities and aptitude to produce it's better to stay away from the film business. You won't be happy.

All successful producers have the ability to know (most of the time) what films or videos will succeed with audiences. They have some practical understanding or sixth sense about what works and what doesn't that goes beyond a personal desire to tell a story.

Script Development

Besides this sixth sense—which many may argue is an acquired skill or an inherited ability—the producer must also have the business and persuasive skills to be able to attract, negotiate and eventually acquire literary properties, screenplays, life stories, and other properties that, once produced, will be marketable.

Producers spend much of their time trying to ferret out good scripts, develop relationships with writers, or develop stories into treatments, and treatments into first–, second–, and third–draft screenplays. The first and foremost job of a producer is to find and develop screenplays for films or properties for home video.

This is all done with an eye toward production. For without a property, the producer isn't even at the starting line.

Development is a very high-risk business. It is also expensive. It may cost $100,000 to acquire and develop a property that no one wants to buy. The producer can spend a great deal of money on living expenses while looking for properties. Once a property is found the producer may have to come up with more money to "option" a book, article, screenplay, or life story. An option buys the producer time to begin to assemble a package around the property, including director, actors and financing. But **without a property, nothing happens**. There is nowhere to go. Nothing to do.

Studios have development and story departments with large staffs of "readers" and story analysts that do nothing but read and evaluate screenplays day in and day out. In a year a studio might read 5,000 screenplays and write as many evaluations or "coverage." Those synopses and screenplay evaluations deemed worthy rise through the development department in the hope they will interest a director and producer. The studios spend millions of dollars to find and develop properties each year. The beginning producer is at a great disadvantage. He does not have the time, staff or resources to hit and miss. He must find something to produce fast or he's not a producer. And it better be good.

How does the producer find properties? It can happen in any number of ways. It can be a book, an article, a life story, or a screenplay draft or treatment. The producer may write the screenplay. Most important is that the property can be made into a good motion picture. In order to find properties the producer must have well-connected friends and associates who can send him material. **A relationship with a small (or large) literary agency or agent can be very valuable.** An agent who believes a producer can really get the job done will supply scripts for the producer to read. After all, the agent's job is to make a sale. The producer also must make friends with lots of screenwriters.

Meanwhile, there is still the problem of how a producer is able to live while all this reading, searching, meeting, and lunching takes place. Some producers raise "development money" which enables them to live (for a little while), pay writers, and have money with which to option properties. Nothing, however is more risky than development because most properties don't ever get made. The money spent for development may never even have a chance of being returned. Because the risk is so high, the producer who does raise development money must not only repay investors but give them a very healthy return on their investment. In some development deals, once the film is financed the producer will repay investors plus a large return on

31

their money in order to "buy them out." That is, the investor is paid off and doesn't participate in the film's earnings. He's already made his profit. **This buyout allows the producer to protect his future upside should the film be successful.** Other deals allow the investor the choice to convert the development investment into "profit participation" in the film itself. This can severely cut into a producer's profits later on but is a fair way of rewarding the investor.

Whenever you use someone else's money and the risk is high, so is the return that you have to pay. That is why many producers prefer to find ways to take on the burden of development themselves. When a property is sold or produced, they own it and reap the rewards.

Script Development Deals

Some producers go to the studios for "development deals." This is very common. The studios produce less than one for every fifty scripts that are developed. If the studio says "no" after paying for development it's possible that this is the end of the story. Unless the producer's lawyer has negotiated a "turnaround deal"—which means that if the film doesn't go into production in some period of time (six months, one year) the producer is free to take the script elsewhere for production financing. In this case the studio gets to recoup its development costs (and sometimes overhead and interest) when the script (which the studio funded) is bought by another studio or financier. The studio may also get some small percentage of profits as well. Without a turnaround clause a film may forever be stuck in a studio.

Unless there's a turnaround clause in the contract the project will end up in a dusty studio library where no one can get his hands on it. This is because a studio development deal is usually done as a step deal. The studio has approvals all along the way—usually at different drafts. At every step the studio can decide to stop the development. It is not uncommon for an executive who initiated the development deal to be

32

gone in 18 months while the script is still in development. The next executive may have no interest in the script because he or she will want to develop his or her own projects. Besides, if the film were ever made and it was a success, the previous executive would get the credit. If the film fails, the new executive would be blamed. What usually happens is the new executive will cancel the development deal and the producer is forced to start all over again.

Note: Studio deals are really outside the scope of this book because the assumption is made the producers will be making films at less-than-studio budgets and will want to retain creative control. When a studio develops a script it will make the creative decisions about how the film will be packaged and will control every element from production through editing and marketing.

Somehow our producer has survived the development process. The producer has figured out a way to live, has found a terrific property, has negotiated the option, and commissioned a screenplay. What other resources will the producer need to move closer to financing?

Packaging

A good package. One technique that producers have used in tandem to elevate their screenplays and help a buyer "see" the finished film is to **develop key art or a poster for the film (before it's been made!)**. Sometimes it's just the key art, or a title treatment or even a poster. This art work conveys a strong sense of what the film will be about. The marketing hooks are clearly established in the art work, which generates excitement among potential distributors and investors alike.

Since the poster art (billboards), key art (as seen in newspaper ads) or package art (video cassette covers) is really the first, and maybe the only thing that people see—before seeing the movie itself—it makes sense that producers are using this technique to help sell their film. **However, if a producer does not have the resources and know-**

how to get a strong piece of art work prepared it's better not to do it. If he creates a bad piece of art, he hurts rather than helps his project. This happens all the time. It's amazing how many producers aren't able to visualize very well and won't employ professional theatrical poster designers.

Video producers also frequently prepare art work for their projects prior to production. I have seen more dreadful key art treatments than I care to remember. I can't believe it. These producers are suppose to be visual people. The problem may be that producers don't know how to commission and oversee art work. They may think they've got something terrific, but usually it's just the reverse. Preparing key art is the job of the marketing department, which employs a creative services department which in turn selects several designers, art directors, and illustrators to carry out the design work.

There are really very few designers, illustrators, and art directors that know how to design key art for movies and video cassette packaging. It's a unique art form unto itself and should not be undertaken by amateurs, or even professional designers who work in other fields. If you go this route, you are asking for trouble. If you can assemble the right team to prepare key art, that engages investors and distributors, it will be a great boost to your selling efforts. If you can't, don't try it. The cost for artwork can be as little as a few thousand dollars or as much as $25,000, depending on who is commissioned to do the illustration and design work.

Producers such as Dino DeLaurentis, Roger Corman and Charlie Band have pre-sold foreign territory rights based on the art work alone without a frame of film being shot. In fact, on a regular basis Charlie Band would make sales calls to Vestron's film department with a large stack of posterboards under his arm. If the key executives liked what they saw they would commission the development of a film. At that time, video cassette packaging was often more important than what was in the box, and hence the attention to key art.

Support Team

You can't do it alone. "Independent" producers are really "dependent" on many, many other people. Producers can't begin to do all the jobs necessary to complete a motion picture or video program themselves. A core team is essential. Most producers will develop long-term relationships over their careers with creative partners, lawyers and accountants.

Sales Person

There are all kinds of producers. Some producers are better at finding properties than they are pitching to investors, distributors, and banks. If you know your own strengths (and weaknesses) it saves an enormous amount of time because you can partner with someone who has a skill that you may lack. If you are a poor salesperson, find a charismatic talker who enjoys selling, pitching and presenting the project. Conversely if you are better at presentations but weak on identifying good projects, find a partner who is a master sleuth in finding properties. **Investments are often made as much in the people involved in a project as in the actual project itself.** People are a project's greatest asset because it is the people who bring the ideas in the script to life.

Lawyer

A lawyer is a key player in the production of motion pictures and videos. A lawyer is involved in drafting the numerous agreements that are part of the business of producing films and videos. These include options on properties and screenplays, insurance contracts, completion bonds, corporate structuring, distribution and limited partnership contracts, agent contracts, and agreements with unions, stars, banks and many others. Once you start getting commitments, your lawyer can begin to formalize these agreements. The agreements must all dovetail so that everything, from the money to the actor's schedules, will be ready at the right time. Find an entertainment attorney that you like who is well versed in the field.

Accountant

An accountant will work closely with the lawyer and will consult on many key financial structural issues, such as taxes. Your accountant should be an entertainment accountant well-versed in tax issues. Remember, too, it's your accountant that will instigate audits with distributors, should this be necessary.

Production Company

If you don't have a production company you may want to join forces with a production company that has previously produced films or videos. Production companies have numerous contacts among the professionals that handle physical production. They have forms and accounting procedures and can function in many other areas that will keep you from having to reinvent the wheel. An experienced production company will also give you, your investors, the completion bond company, and your distributor a sense of comfort.

Rights Package—Letters of Intent

In your arsenal of resources will be various agreements. If you go out into the world and represent that you have a particular star or director or production company or line producer or law/accounting firm or screenplay writer, then you better have who you say you have. Document this in a contract or in a letter of intent which says, based on their schedule the pertinent person/firm will participate with you. These documents give your buyers and investors a strong sense that your project will take place as you've said it will. You will be raising money and making distribution and pre-sales deals based upon these commitment letters. Your ability to do so will be only as strong as the commitments of your key players.

Financial Package

Determine the financial vehicle that you will use to raise your financing. This may take one of a variety of forms: a limited partnership, a general partnership, a joint venture, a corporation or a non-profit foundation. You probably want to have your financial structure in place prior to raising any money. That way, you can readily accept financing when you find it. On the other hand, the contributor of the financing may have a preference for one form over another. If his contribution is large enough it may alter the financial structure itself. That's why it's important to have a pretty good idea of how you will structure your financing and where you expect to get your money. Whatever the structure, this will be indicated in your prospectus and/or sales presentations so that potential funders know exactly how things are set up.

Your financing strategy may change once you actually get into the marketplace. Your ability to strike a pre-sale deal or a negative pick-up (where a distributor makes payment for your picture upon completion) will significantly change where you need to go for the balance of your financing. As you assemble all the elements for your production, **you should probably have a financing structure clearly in mind** and prepared for you by your lawyer. (This book will give you some options on where you may obtain your financing and how you might piece it together. Your financial structure will come out of the options that you think you have available to you. Consult your accountant and lawyer before proceeding with setting up your structure.)

Budget

A critical element in your package will be a professionally prepared budget. Without a budget you won't really know what to raise, nor will you be able to justify your budget if anyone asks—and they will! Many producers back into their budgets. In other words, they think about how much they can raise and then they create a budget to match that figure. This is not the right way to go about it. Prepare your budget based on the final-draft screenplay you intend to produce. From your screenplay, the production manager who prepares your budget can determine the below-the-line or hard costs. Below-the-line is the real cost of physical production based on the script. The variables will come from above-the-line fees, which are for actors, producers, and directors. You won't know exactly what the above-the-line fees will be until deals with actors are actually negotiated. You may have an idea but you won't know exactly.

Your budgets must be realistic. They must reflect real, standard costs and demonstrate that the production is highly professional. Don't include all your special side deals and savings in your budget. If they fall through, then you will be undercapitalized. It's better to **have a legitimate budget prepared by an experienced production manager** than a budget that looks too low. Studios, distributors, and sometimes your investors will be scared off if they spot a substandard budget. Why not be a hero later, when you finish your film under budget?

At Vestron I reviewed hundreds of budgets. Many revealed the inexperience of the producer. Budgets that were too thin, or full of omissions or oversights, sent up red flags. Distributors, studios, and financiers want only to work with someone who is fiscally responsible and can get the job done.

Financiers, be they private individuals, distributors or bankers, will probably insist on a completion bond company that acts as an insurance company. Should you go over budget, the investors won't be required to put in more money because, for a fee, the completion bond company assumes this risk. (If you look as if you are going over budget they may take over the completion of the project.) Your budget items will be reviewed line by line by the completion bond company; unless they approve it (and probably add 10 percent contingency to it) they won't insure the production. They have to think that you've got enough money to shoot the film depicted in your script.

Banks know that the release costs (marketing and publicity) are the same for a low- or high-budget film (assuming they both play in the same number of theaters). The studios would rather spend print and ad dollars on a large "A" film with top stars that they know will draw an audience. For this reason studio distribution will be very difficult to obtain, so you may want to raise money independently for print and advertising (which can be in the millions) should you not find a distributor willing to front these costs.

Money-Saving Tips

Saving money is the same as having money. It also means that you don't have to raise money nor give profit participation for that money to investors for taking a risk.

Finding money-cutting techniques for your production is another form of financing, except this time you don't have to ask anybody for anything. You just have to be resourceful. **Every dollar you save is a dollar you don't have to raise.** Here are a few ways to enhance your project and save money:

• Re-use sets. Find a studio or producer who has just completed a film. Recycle and redress their sets and you won't have the expense of designing and building original sets.

• Co-produce with someone who has a successful track record. Use his credits to boost the integrity and the appeal of your package.

• Raise some money through grants, or development investments, or pre-buys. Having some money puts you in a more credible position with distributors, rights buyers, and other investors. No one likes to contribute the first money.

• Make a deal with a lab or video facility. Make them a partner in the profits of the film for supplying the film, processing, or video post-production on the project.

• Use film festivals as a way to get a distributor's attention (if you don't already have one). Employ a sales rep or a film publicist, or both, to help you.

• Create long-term relationships with your investors. This means keeping them informed. When something good happens, call them, or send them a letter or fax. Invite them to screenings. Pay back their money, even if it's only a little at a time. You want to build up loyalty. If you're in it for the long haul and you treat your investors right, they may be in it for the long haul too. Make deals that benefit your investors before yourself and you'll have their support forever.

• Make deals with the unions. Don't be afraid to call them and negotiate. If you use SAG (Screen Actor's Guild) actors and shoot a low-budget film you can get special rates on films under $500,000 or $1,500,000.

• Deal. Deal. Deal. **A good line producer lives to negotiate.**

He negotiates for everything. From hotel rooms to food to rental cars to props, locations, and lab work to crew salaries. Everything is negotiable. There's simply no other way to do it and get the most money on the screen. Hiring an experienced unit manager or line producer is one of the best things you can do. He can save you substantially more than you pay him. Give him a bonus whenever he saves you money.

Deferred Payment

Deferrals are one way to reduce the up-front financing required. However, unless you, the cast, and crew all agree to defer your fees, morale problems may arise on the set if some people get paid and others don't. The problem with deferrals is that unless the film makes a profit no one gets paid. And since most films don't make a profit...

Income Projections

Most income projections are fantasy, even when presented as "low," "medium," and "high." Who really knows what your film or video will net? There are so many factors—positive and negative—beyond your and your distributor's control. Nevertheless, it's the one page that all investors and financial people will want to see. You can help create a successful picture by compiling box office grosses of films that **are similar in genre and budget to the one you are proposing**. (Don't get carried away here. When I say "similar" I mean similar. NINJA TURTLES isn't similar, okay?) It makes no sense to compare your picture to mega-hit pictures. It's better to pick a dozen substantial films (or videos) really similar to your own in genre and budget level that have been released in recent years.

Most budgets are too low. Most income projections are too high. The discrepancy between the two quickly shatters investors' expectations. It's very easy to write high-income projections, but if they don't pan out you'll suffer when you try to raise money again and find doors closed. It's better to keep expectations low and be a hero later.

Note: I'm hitting on this point particularly hard because 75 percent of the income projections and budgets I've seen for independent films and videos are not only overly optimistic but embarrassingly amateurish and demonstrate the producers have little understanding of costs and sales potentials. Investors are in their right minds for running in the opposite direction.

The more you understand how other films have been sold and marketed, the more clout you will have with your financial people when you make your projections. Having had a past success in the film or video business certainly helps your expertise and credibility. Put enough substantial information together to allow the investor to imagine that your film is clearly in line as the next breakthrough. Then let them dream.

Do your homework and calculate the profit potential of a film from all sources: include foreign, television, cable, and home video as well as theatrical. Since the domestic theatrical success greatly affects the income you will see from other markets you should make sure that your projections indicate these connections. You may need help in creating these projections. Nothing looks worse than projections that are clearly made up and have no basis in reality in terms of the assumptions used.

If you've prepared a realistic budget and income projections and you learn there is little or no chance of making the money back on the film, then it's probably better not to seek investors who expect a financial return. Breaking even is not what it's about if you have investors. Looking for grants—you don't have to pay the money back and there aren't investors looking for a return on their investment—is probably a better way to go.

What you want to do is assemble a package that has not only a good chance of breaking even (because there are numerous ancillary revenue streams) but also has an upside potential. You want to reward your investors handsomely, which will put you in the catbird's seat for your next picture.

Completion Bonds

The bank will certainly require a completion bond so that completion of the film will be guaranteed. The completion bond is an insurance policy (for your investors, the bank, the distributors, and others). If the film goes over budget the guarantor finishes the film or gives the producer monies necessary to complete it. The guarantor keeps a watchful eye on the progress of the film throughout production via the daily production reports. A bank that will help finance your production will demand a completion guarantee as security. There are only a few completion bond companies that are credible to banks.

Completion bonds usually cost 6 percent of the budget (although 50 percent of this charge might be rebated if the film comes in on budget. The completion bond company—which is really in the insurance business—will probably also sell cast and crew insurance, E&O (errors and omission) insurance, negative insurance, etc., along with the completion bond.

With an armload of insurance policies and completion bonds, you may start to get the feeling that everyone is looking out for his own investment by assuming a worst-case scenario and making sure his downside is protected. You're right. This theme will be replayed in every financial relationship you'll have. You'll get used to it and come to expect it. In fact, **it's the producer's job to provide as much protection for everyone as possible.**

Lab Deals

You may find a film lab (or a video production facility) that will provide services in exchange for a share in the upside profits after the film has recouped its costs. For example, a film lab may provide your film prints (at nearly $2,000 a print times 500 theaters—a moderate release—the total is approximately $1 million). A lab deal can provide part of your P&A and perhaps allow you to strike a better deal with your film distributor, which now won't have to pay for prints. The deal with the lab might give it 25 percent of gross receipts until the prints are recouped, then 5 percent until the budget of the film is recouped and then 10 percent thereafter. This may be too expensive a deal to make if the film has a tremendous upside. On the other hand, it's a million dollars you don't have to raise, and this also means you don't have to find a distributor willing to pay for prints.

Advertising Deals

These deals are probably few and far between but if you are really creative, you might find a large advertising company with lots of barter media time on its hands (print, radio, and television). Perhaps it would be willing to convert its media time into equity in your film. The barter costs the advertising company 40 percent of the book rate of the media so if your film repays the ad firm's investment easily, it makes a profit. Of course, if the company is able to sell its bartered media easily, that's a far less risky proposition than making a deal with you.

Distribution

The primary asset in your financing package will be the distributor. A distributor brings comfort to investors. Many filmmakers, however, are willing to take a chance, make their film without a distributor in place—assuming it will be absolutely fabulous—and then try to create a bidding war among distributors for the highest advance. If your investors can stand the risk and don't need the guarantee of a distributor **and** you are an excellent producer with a strong script, spectacular cast, **and** you know what you are doing **then** you might be able to pull this off. It's only for the strong-hearted, and only the most successful producers are able to make this formula work.

More likely, you will be looking for a distributor from day one. The good news is that they will all see you. No one—including the studios—will want to miss an opportunity. They all need pictures. They all have acquisition staffs that track the scripts being written and the films going into production. The competition is very, very tough. Distributors evaluate projects all day long. Even still, you'll get your shot. **But you'll only get one, so it's important that your package is as strong as you can possibly make it.** You must convince the distributor of the merit of your project in order to add him to your package.

If you find that you can't get to the studios directly, then you'll need a well-connected agent who can open doors for you. The agent will receive a fee only when your film is sold. Representation will not cost you anything up front.

If you are at the package stage, everything should be very well organized and presented. You will make the best impression and create the greatest value for your uncompleted film by having assembled the resources discussed in this chapter.

Note: Most producers are more focused on the other jobs of producing and don't look toward marketing, not realizing that a "green light" decision on a picture may come from its marketability.

(For information about marketing films and videos see Wiese's books, *Film and Video Marketing* and *Home Video: Producing for the Home Market*.)

The Role of Banks

Banks are used in many motion picture (and sometimes video) production deals. Producers who utilize banks do so because they find it's cheaper to use a bank's money. The bank usually doesn't take an equity share in the film or video—and that's good news for producers who are taking the risk. The bank turns to the producer for the repayment of the loan. The producer is vulnerable to the loss of house, cars, capital, and property should the loan default. High rollers like Francis Coppola and Vestron founder Austin Furst mortgaged their homes to launch films and a video distribution company, respectively.

Distributors use banks when they pre-buy films. Banks are also used by investors who will borrow money on a producer's behalf by putting up a letter of credit. By doing so, the investor is personally guaranteeing that—if the producer defaults—the investor will make good on the loan. No actual money leaves the hands of either the distributor or the investor but each is on the hook with the bank—not the producer. He, of course, is on the hook with the distributor and investor but is not liable to the bank directly.

There are no standard distribution contracts even though distributors will always tell you *"This is our standard deal."* Standard distribution contracts favor them, not you. The same is true with financing agreements. There are no standard contracts: everyone makes his or her own deals. This is where you need expert advice from your lawyer and accountant in order to determine the meaning of the terms and language used in the contracts. **It is extremely important that the definitions of the terms used have the same meaning for both the producer and financing entity.** (Your lawyer earns his or her fee defining and clarifying the meaning of your deal!)

Bankers

Bankers are conservative. This is their job. They don't want to be in the business of taking risks, so they don't. Unlike your investors, creative partners, actors and other show-biz people, bankers are not swayed by your "great scripts" or "fabulous projects." Your most exuberant pitch won't elicit much emotion. You must understand what the banks are looking for in order to garner a response and give you a loan. Your pitch to your banker must come from an entirely different context.

Your package—the screenplay, actors, a director, and possibly, a distribution deal—is the product that you are selling. Your buyers are bankers, investors, distribution companies, pay TV, and foreign distributors—all of which will invest money or give you bankable deals for the money to make your film. In selling your package you must make it as attractive as you can to these very sophisticated buyers. Your presentation must assure them that **it will meet their needs and expectations.**

Banks are interested in assessing whether you (and your partners, distributors, foreign sales agents) are a good risk. *What's in the banker's mind is, what kind of return will the bank make if it loans you money? Do you and your partners have enough assets to make good on the loan? Is your budget realistic? Is your distribution plan realistic? Will it spin off the kind of revenues you project? What if it doesn't? Are there contingencies and other revenue streams or guarantees that the bank can count on? Do you have iron-clad agreements with reputable partners?* They won't give your fabulous key art concept a moment's glance; your net worth is what gets their juices flowing. Always remember: **Banks are interested in making safe, risk-free loans.** They don't care how great your film is going to be. Your job is to bring them a sense of comfort when you make your presentation. If you can't do that, either you're not well prepared or you don't understand that the bank requires an entirely different presentation than any other institution along the financing path.

Bank Loans

The good news about bank loans is that they are the best of all arrangements because you don't have to give any profit participation to the bank. The bad news is that you have to have a strong enough financial statement (or pre-buy agreements) and leverage to get the bank to loan you money, which will cost 2 or 3 points above the prevailing prime rate.

A second good feature about a bank loan is that because you are not dependent on a distributor for financing, you should be able to cut a better deal with your distributor. If he finances the film, he will want a 30 to 35 percent distribution fee. If you finance the film and assume a greater risk, his fee may be reduced from 20 to 25 percent, which increases your upside potential.

With a loan, however, someone (possibly you) is on the line to pay it back. In addition, the bank will require some kind of guarantee that could be a personal guarantee (a second mortgage as collateral) or negative pick-up or pre-sale agreement that you have with "bankable" companies.

What's "Bankable"?

"Bankable" agreements will vary depending on the bank's requirements, which will usually be very tough. The bank wants to be sure that your contract is with a reputable company that, 18 months from now, will be liquid enough to make the promised payments. The bank will make sure that the company has not overextended its financial commitments. The bank is looking for a distribution company that it can trust to make payments to it upon delivery of the film.

It's almost impossible to ask what's "bankable" because you will get different answers from every bank. Once you find a bank that you like, you can pose the question and understand its requirements. Producers think that some stars are "bankable" only to find out their bank doesn't think a star's appearance in a film will make any difference. Other producers may assume that distribution and pre-buy agreements with top-notch companies are bankable, only to come face to face with a banker who knows how hard domestic distribution is for independents. The bank will know that in recent years a producer can't depend entirely on theatrical returns to pay back a loan. In fact, many independent theatrical films do not even recoup their print and advertising costs from theatrical exhibition. Banks also know the importance of a domestic theatrical release and its effect on the value of the film in the ancillary markets. They know too that there can be a lag period of from 12 to 18 months between a film's domestic release and its foreign release and exploitation. A bank will also look to television or home video distribution to repay its loans. Or worse yet, the bank may not consider any of these contracts and markets worthy of their loan and may turn instead to the borrower's real estate or personal assets.

The bank is not in the film business. Most don't want to be in the film business. They know how risky it is. If a producer defaults on a loan what are they going to do with a warehouse of film? Banks would rather have a producer's house, car and coin collection.

The Banks

Banks who financed motion pictures (mostly with the studios) are the "entertainment divisions" of Bank of America, First National Bank of Boston, Bankers Trust, Chase Manhattan, Chemical, Continental Illinois, Crocker, First National Bank of Chicago, Credit Lyonnais Bank Netherlands and Securities Pacific.

Each bank has different requirements, which change frequently. Chemical Bank, one of the largest film financiers, will want the producer to put up from 10 to 30 percent of the budget in cash with collateral for the balance, plus interest payments. Chemical Bank may accept foreign pre-buy contracts (based on who the buyer is) supported by letters of credit from the buyer's domestic bank. They may ask that the producer defer his fees as well as all above-the-line fees (using the deferred fees to pay the interest on the loan). In every deal, banks will always be looking out for themselves first.

European American Bank (EAB) is another bank known for film financing, but only to producers who have track records. They may look to the producer's share of profits in the film as collateral for foreign and cable pre-sales.

Frans Afman heads up the Credit Lyonnais Bank Netherlands, another major lender. There are over 35 people in the film division. Traditionally, motion picture financing was served by American banks but many left the field in the early 1980s because they wanted to be fully secured before making loans. Credit Lyonnais came in and picked up a lot of business that was left by the American banks.

Credit Lyonnais Bank wants a producer's film to have a major studio domestic release, foreign contracts and a completion bond before lending money. De Laurentiis was financed by Credit Lyonnais in his heyday. The bank does not make loans on a project basis but will make credit loans based on assets like film libraries. This requirement eliminates many independents who don't own their films. Wall Street was the first to start to look to film library assets as the collateral for loans, and the banks followed.

Each deal is different, and a bank's desire to provide motion picture financing changes constantly. It's best to begin discussions with banks who have done film financing to understand today's requirements. Contact banks early and learn what their requirements are. It can be a long process and may take up to a half year or more to meet all the bank's requirements and have your pre-buy and distribution contracts in order. It may also cost many tens of thousands of dollars in legal fees, depending on the complexity of the loan and supplemental agreements. In recent years, banks have begun to look for ownership in films other than a producer's interest payments. Regardless of how staunch a bank may look and how tough a front it may present— **everything is negotiable**. You may not end up signing the banking agreement that was first presented when you walked in the door.

Banking Strategy

Banks are in business to do business. They want to make loans, but only loans they feel comfortable making. They want long term relationships and will be interested in working with you to finance all your future films. A one-shot project is far less interesting to a bank than establishing a relationship for your future business ventures. If you (and your partners) appear to be a good risk, bankers will want to do business with you. They want to loan you money every year of your career because the more they loan you, the greater their interest collections. The bank will also like to spread its risk over all your projects, not just one, hoping that if one picture fails, another will cover the loan and interest payments. In some regards, a producer's goals and a banker's goals are really very similar. Both want to

51

establish long-term relationships. Neither wants to have to qualify the other with every new project. Both want to cut through the start-up delays and getting-to-know-you stage in order to put a financing deal in place.

It's nearly impossible to specify what banks want these days because the business has been so volatile. Like it or not, you (or your lawyer or accountant) will have to do a lot of footwork to test the banking marketplace when it comes time to finance your project. Bank deals change daily. This requires that you be flexible and very creative in how you put your deals together.

Summary

This is an overview of some of the major resources that you'll need to put in place as you begin the financing journey. Obviously, the higher the budget the more elaborate the package, because there is more at risk. Feature films will require significantly more packaging than home videos, but almost all of these elements and resources are common to both kinds of projects.

Key Resources: Summary

• Your team's development ability is top-notch. This will be reflected in the property you've selected to produce. The script should be excellent, in final draft form, and ready for production.

• You have an entertainment lawyer and accountant who will review and negotiate any serious offers you may get.

• You have an agent who will open doors with distributors for you and can, along with your lawyer, negotiate in your behalf.

• You have commitments from a director and well-known stars that will increase the market value and promotability of the film.

• You have (or have an alliance with) a production company that is well-known and has a strong track record. This will give a distributor and financiers the necessary confidence and quell any questions about quality and the producer's ability to deliver the final film.

• If you have already obtained some financing—great! The more locked in it is, the better. This financing could be from:
- family and friends
- investors
- foreign pre-sales
- negative pick-up or guarantee
- bankable contracts or letters of credit.

• You have a realistic budget.

• You have realistic income projections based on realistic market assumptions. Income projections are usually not given to distributors since they mean less to a distributor who will assess the film's value on their own. They'll do this by polling their sales and marketing executives and projecting what they think the picture will do in a variety of markets. They'll prepare their own marketing plan and analysis of your picture before they make you an offer.

If you are asking a distributor to make an equity investment in the project and you have other equity partners (such as foreign sales agents or video companies) and can provide the distributor with expected revenues based on your equity partners' input, income projections will be appropriate in your presentation.

• A completion bond company will be in place.

• A video facilities deal has been explored.

• A lab deal for prints or a deal for advertising or a video facilities deal has been explored. If you are able to bring this to a distributor it will be most welcome and unexpected.

• Prepare first-class key art and lead copy lines that will communicate to the distributor the marketing angle for the picture. The more appealing they are, the more people will want to see the picture, and the more it will be worth to distributors and investors alike. The more mass oriented your film is, as opposed to its being an art film, the easier it will be to sell. The promotable elements should be extremely clear in both your package and the artwork you present. Show artwork only if it is done by a professional.

• Find banks that want to do long-term business with you. Build a relationship. The earlier you start the better. Learn your bank's requirements, then design your presentation accordingly.

RISK CAPITAL

RISK CAPITAL

"Offer a fair deal to your investors and you'll stand head and shoulders above other producers."

Risk Capital: What is it?

Risk capital is speculative money—usually spent on the production of a film or video (and sometimes on the release)—in return for an equity or profit participation in it. Risk capital can come from the producer, his family, friends, investors, foreign and domestic corporations, distributors, co-production partners, a limited partnership of investors, or other joint ventures. It can also take the form of a letter of credit. Or below-the-line and facilities trades for an equity position.

Independent Financing Approaches: Greg Johnson Interview

Greg Johnson, vice president of corporate development for Vestron Pictures, was involved in the financing for a number of Vestron films including DIRTY DANCING, which cost from $6 to $7 million and grossed well over $150 million domestically. (See Wiese's *Film & Video Marketing* for a marketing case study of DIRTY DANCING.) We discussed the producer's path to financing low-budget films.

How does an independent raise financing? How much or how little should he or she look for? What if your friends want to invest?

"You're talking to everybody that you can possibly think of. Your signal flag is definitely up. You are looking for money. You try to cut

57

an <u>equity deal</u> at any cost if you can make a fair deal. And the equity provided is on a sufficient enough scale to justify the costs involved. It's pretty safe to assume that any amount less than $500,000—unless it's coming from a single source—is probably not worth your while. Why is that? The reason is you've got legal fees and probably several lawyers to pay. Why have a lawyer involved? Maybe someone you know is willing to give you $100,000—you've been best friends and he or she wants to support you and invest in your movie. Well, the best of friendships can always be ruined over money or over misunderstandings so you want to record whatever you do. You need to get a lawyer involved to explicitly outline the do's and don'ts. Such as: What are the representations you are making about the film? How the investment is going to be used? How will the investment be recouped? Lawyers produce these documents fairly inexpensively because they do this kind of work all the time. There is no such thing as a 'plain vanilla' financing deal. There is always fine tuning that needs to be done. It costs from about $10,000 to $25,000 to set up a limited partnership to finance a movie."

Let's say that investors are going to put up $1,000,000 toward your budget and that you'll raise the rest from other sources. Give me a model scenario.

"The investors you find aren't going to be friends. They are probably people you've carefully culled from your network who are interested in investing in movies. Let's say you've got a group of four or five individuals who want to put in a million dollars. What is the net benefit to you from that million dollars? First of all, whoever has helped you contact these individuals is going to want to take a cut of it. There are going to be some finder's fees attached, and the typical finder's fee is 10 percent. Now you're down to $900,000. Your legal fees will be somewhere in the neighborhood of from $15,000 to $20,000. So you're down to $880,000. Remember that you are going to have ongoing costs and responsibilities to these investors and you are going to have to bring in an accountant who will report to these investors on an ongoing basis."

What will the limited partnership deal look like?

"There are many, many ways to pay back your investors. As producer you are not going to take a piece of any film revenue until your investors have been recouped in full and been given some premium for the use of their money and for the risk that they incurred by investing in the film. Usually that's a 25 percent premium above the amount invested.

"After the investor has received his money back at a premium, there is usually some sort of revenue-sharing program that allows the producer to take a graduated share in the upside of the film. One way that could work is that after the investors have received 125 percent of their investment, the sharing ratio for the next $1 million might be 25 percent to the producer and the remainder to the investors, and following that corridor it could be 50/50 sharing thereafter. The theory is that you want to allow your investors a reasonable return before you start taking the lion's share of the profits."

LIMITED PARTNERSHIPS

Independent financing through a limited partnership gives the producer much more creative control over all elements of the picture. Limited partners don't watch over the producer's shoulder. They are called "limited partners" for two reasons: first, they don't get involved in the partnership's business (their business role is "limited" to passive investing), and second, their investment is "limited"—they aren't liable for any more money, even if it's needed.

The producer normally sets up a limited partnership with himself (and others) as "general partners," a separate business entity. He then hires a production company to develop and produce the film or video.

Limited partnership structures can be very simple or complex. The most simple models look something like this:

50/50 Model
Limited partners invest
Net receipts from all sources come into partnership
Limited partners are paid back their investment
General and limited partners split balance 50/50

As an incentive to invest some deals will pay back the investors or limited partners with interest before spliting the balance:

50/50 Model with Interest Before Split
Limited partners put up budget (investment)
Net receipts from all sources come into partnership
Limited partners are paid back their investment plus 25%
General and limited partners split balance 50/50

Sometimes the investors are further incentivized by a split that favors them:

40/60 Model with Interest Before Split
Limited partners put up budget (investment)
Net receipts from all sources come into partnership
Limited partners are paid back their investment plus 25%
Split balance: General partners 40%/Limited partners 60%

Or, sometimes the investors are well taken care of in advance of the general partners but should the film really make a profit the generals benefit greatly:

Model with Profit Split Shifts at Performance Levels
Limited partners put up budget (investment)
Net receipts from all sources come into partnership
Limited partners receive 90%,
General partners receive 10% until investment plus 15% is recouped.

Up to the first $2 million (or some number) the Limited partners
receive 70%, the General partners receive 30%.
After $2 million, the formula flips to Limited partners (30%),
General partners (70%)

These are all arbitrary models. You can be very creative in how these
deals are structured. Consult your lawyer. Keep in mind however
that if you can find an appealing structure that is beneficial and fair to
your investors you will have an easier time raising money.

If the limited partnership is set up to finance "development" (creation,
acquisition and writing of scripts), investors recoup their money (and
possibly interest) if and when the producer raises financing. (The cost
of development is included in the budget.) The investors also have
some profit participation in the picture. However, development is an
even riskier investment than film investing because many films that
are developed never get made. At least a finished film has a shot in the
marketplace.

LETTERS OF CREDIT

Sometimes investors don't have to put up any actual money but can
use their own lines of credit to secure financing from their own banks
for the producer. This way the investor doesn't have to liquify assets
in order to invest in your film. Ask investors to give you a *"letter of
credit"* that you can take to the bank to draw cash. The bank charges a
few points of interest for this (which you can have other investors
cover). This way, your investors are not out of pocket. You borrow
money from investors (via the bank) to produce your film, repay
them, and give them profit participation in the net profits of your
films. As the producer, it is your responsibility to repay the bank.

EQUITY INVESTMENTS

Greg Johnson feels "equity" investment is the best of all possible routes:

"Limited partnership money is the type of money that you always want to bring to a film because it is money without any strings attached. It's pure equity investment that goes into the budget of the picture and does not require you to give up any rights. All you are required to do is insure that your investors have a reasonable chance of recoupment and participate in the profits. Equity is the golden ring.

"However, finding film investors is a very difficult process because the golden ring of equity investment is difficult to come by. If you don't come out of an investor environment, you literally have to go out and create the contacts. You have to be visible, you have to talk to bankers, accountants, to anyone that you think will be helpful in connecting you with people who want to invest in film. They are out there, but let's face it, the environment for pure equity money in films is getting more difficult to locate every year because people have been hurt by equity investment in the past. Trying to start out as a producer in search of financing is not an enviable position to be in by any means."

Are there people who raise money for producers?

"There are people who raise money and who have done so successfully. The large Wall Street firms such as Merrill Lynch and the Silver Screen Partnerships have raised hundreds of millions of dollars for motion picture projects.

"The producer with one $2 million dollar picture is at a disadvantage compared to those strong financial and brokerage houses going out

62

with a multi-picture deal for a major studio. The pool available for film financing is finite. You've got to realize that even though you are a producer you're basically trying to go after that same pool of money. You are competing against major companies with well-established financing programs that have been groomed by some of the biggest institutions in the world."

An independent seeking to finance his or her first film isn't going to go to Wall Street.

"Exactly. Without a track record you don't have much to sell the public. Selling limited partnerships is as much selling the people behind the partnerships as it is the deal. You also can't offer diversification."

So, a small independent producer looks to friends, family, and "believers."

"The best way to go is to bring your investors in not as investors but as 'partners.' If you're going to be able to raise money outside of your family and friends and if Wall Street is closed to you, then you are really bringing in people who, for various reasons, want to invest in motion pictures. They like the project, they like the sex appeal—whatever the reason, they have decided to invest in your picture. So it behooves you not to treat or think of those people as passive investors but as financial partners in your picture. And the fewer people, the better."

Would you recommend setting up your limited partnership at the same time as you are trying to sell to distributors?

"You're always talking to distribution. You have to assume your project is not going to be financed by a limited partnership because the odds are against you. If you can make a sale, terrific—it puts you that much closer to getting your film produced.

63

"If you've acquired a property (and unless you are a well-known, successful producer with Japanese partners behind you), or producing for a major studio that has limited partnership money available to it already in place it will be a long shot to raise limited partnership money. There are special situations in which you can look across borders to Europe, to Canada, to countries where *blocked funds* (see the Blocked Funds chapter) exist that are available to you. But if you are an average producer doing your first project, the *pre-sale* (see the Pre-Sale chapter) route is going to be the easiest way to go by far."

It's very tough just starting out. Your family is paying your rent. You don't know investors. The distributors have never heard of you. You have little or nothing to show—just a lot of intention.

"The most important thing is that you are networking, telling everyone you know about your project, beginning to open doors for yourself. So you aren't really just starting with a telephone and a script, you're talking to everyone you know about what you are doing and circulating it to agents. A whole constellation of people out there can help you: agents who want to place their stars; lawyers who put together deals for a living, who have terrific contacts and want to represent you if you have a good project; accountants who work like lawyers and agents in putting people together. **I think visibility is as important as anything**. The idea is to get your property into as many hands as possible."

If our first-time producer has very few contacts, what does he do?

"You want to find people who can open doors for you with potential rights buyers. I am not talking about people who help you package the film. No one likes to make the cold call to HBO or the CBS/FOX acquisition department when he is a nobody. His calls don't get returned. As a first time producer you are trying to get over that hurdle and legitimizing what you are doing by getting some buzz and awareness going for you."

So maybe he should find a friendly lawyer who is willing to help because he likes the producer and/or his project.

"You are going to be moving on both fronts, packaging and financing. You are going to need a foreign sales rep—someone who has a deep enough Rolodex to contact buyers. Or better yet, someone to take your film to film festivals and markets or to sell foreign rights on a pre-sale basis to a single foreign rights sales company in the U.S. You access foreign reps the same way you access HBO. (See Appendix for a list of foreign sales representatives.)

"You have a lot of guys out there who are eager for product because there's a dearth of product right now and output relationships are very hard to come by. You have some who are eager and want to access acquisition people to read your project and will try to get as high an advance from them as possible."

Since independents don't have the clout or contacts to raise large sums of money, they are better off trying to finance very low budget films the first time out?

"Only if you pass the acid test, which is 'who are you?' Are you someone who can be trusted to provide a return on your investment? If you don't have that track record any budget will give you a very difficult marketing problem to overcome."

Is the notion then to team up with a co-producer, or property holder or star?

"Yes and no. Does having a strong producer as your partner help you raise money? I think it opens more doors for you. But does it make you better equipped to raise $15 or $20 million? What you are really doing is passing off the marketing problem to your partner. The question then becomes 'is he strong enough to support a $3- to $5-million dollar offer?' And it's very, very difficult—unless you have a strong track record or some other type of unique selling proposition to make to the investors, the Wall Street route is virtually closed."

Does that mean a novice independent producer is limited to going to family and friends, dentists and doctors?

"What you want to do is build your network. Let's go back to the example of bringing in a co-producer. If I am someone who has a good project and I'm a first time producer and I want to maintain some control over the project by raising equity, I am almost virtually certain to need someone or a group of people around me with friends and contacts that can broaden my network. You have to cast a very broad net in order to bring in a group—albeit a small one—of equity investors. The goal should never be to try to raise 100 percent of your budget from equity. If you can cover anywhere from a quarter to a third of your budget through equity, you have enough substance behind you to go out and put together distribution deals. This enables you to get the remaining monies."

Equity Capital

New models of financing are emerging that combine pre-buys and equity. It's not uncommon today for television buyers, who normally put up a pre-sale sum for television rights, to also ask and get an equity position in the project. On the international front, buyers no longer wish to look at themselves as ancillary sellers but as equity partners. They realize their money is getting pictures made so they ask themselves, *"Why should I buy just a set of rights when the same dollar might also get me a piece of the whole picture?"*

Not only do the buyers get some value for their money, but they get an upside should the project throw off some profits. Some of these deals can work. In such cases, the producer can make a sale and finance his project at the same time. However, he probably doesn't explore this kind of deal, which requires he give away equity, until he's investigated other avenues.

The new strategy in recent years is to identify international corporations that have some ability to buy or sell film product. They may be serving one or more markets with film, and may take equity positions in a picture for which they finance a significant portion of the budget. These sales take time, must be done very slowly and carefully, and need elaborate business plans and financial models. Unlike private investors, corporations do not shoot from the hip and are interested in whether the alliance will generate an attractive rate of return. They'll have the same considerations (and maybe more) as with any other corporate investment.

The emerging trend seems to be an alliance between multinational companies (like Sony and JVC) and highly visible producers (like Guber/Peters and Larry Gordon) who are knowledgeable and have strong hands-on experience with proven studio track records. Some multinational companies may finance independent films as an entry into the film business, testing the waters with hands-on niche producers (e.g., Jarmusch's MYSTERY TRAIN). Although these kinds of deals are not going to be made by first timers, it's important to see where the future of film financing may be headed. You can be sure that the Hollywood financial community is analyzing international corporations that have the ability to buy, sell, broadcast, or merchandise product.

How International "Pre-Buy Equities" Work

Richard Lorber is a principal in Fox/Lorber, a foreign sales agent. He sees the pre-buy equity position as desirable, particularly since it's assumed that the pre-sale will be larger than a simple licensing deal because the buyer is also receiving some equity. It may be a tough pill to swallow for the producer, but he's got to make a deal in order to finance his picture.

Does a producer really want to make what was once a licensing deal and end up giving away equity as well?

"Well, I believe it can be desirable. Whether it's realistic or not is another matter. It's most desirable when there's some equity component. The equity component can be attached to a foreign pre-sale when a foreign buyer puts up a larger share of the total budget than the license fee for that territory and gets all exclusive rights (e.g., theatrical, TV, home video) in that territory, possibly a buy-out (with no future monies owed the producer from distribution), an equity stake in the worldwide distribution, and in some cases shares in the distribution revenue."

Give me an example of how you've seen this work.

"Let's say a Japanese company comes in to finance an entire $3 million budget and retain worldwide distribution rights. If this company wants to distribute only in Japan it puts up 10 percent of the $3 million as a license for 'all rights Japan' because Japan represents approximately 10 percent of the worldwide revenues. So that's $300,000 as a license fee on an all rights basis for Japan, which is very cheap. Then it might come back to put up an additional $700,000 for a 25-percent equity interest in the film.

"At this point the producer has sold all rights in Japan and given up a 25-percent equity in the picture, in return for which he has covered one-third of the budget. This provides tremendously favorable leverage in finding other partners or in making additional pre-sales that leave the producer additional distribution rights plus some reasonable percentage of equity."

Lorber's equity pre-buy model is interesting because it gives the buyer an additional incentive to buy the film. However, 25 percent might not be the right number because normally—in limited partnerships, for example—the money gets 50 percent and the creative gets 50 percent. In Lorber's model, someone putting up a third of the cash gets one-fourth equity instead of one-sixth which might be the share in a limited partnership. On the other hand, the producer is getting a deal and can use it to leverage other deals. He or she can still sell the rest of the world rights and has a third of the budget in hand, which brings substance to other buyers and investors.

Besides Japan, Brazil, Argentina, and Chile are touted as being good prospects for equity investments.

CO-PRODUCTIONS

Co-productions are one of the most practical ways to find valuable "other pieces" of the puzzle—pieces that you need anyway—to finance your films and videos. If you take on co-production partners, they share the risk and the potential wealth and you improve your ability to finance your projects. Not only might you be getting production services but distribution outlets as well. These deals are as varied as snowflakes and limited only by the creative imagination of the people putting the deals together. When there are two or more people who want to make it work, it will.

Many independent feature producers, like Ken Badish of The Movie Store, use the "joint venture" concept in which the partners are theatrical, video, and producer. Each puts up a portion of the financing and each shares in revenues from each other's efforts.

Here are a list of potential co-production partners. Review the list and check as many as may be applicable to your own specific project. This will get you thinking about how to find co-production partners.

Co-Production Partners

Private Investors/Consortium
Foreign Governments/Financiers/Corporations
Theatrical Distributors
International Theatrical Distributors
Home Video Suppliers
International Home Video Suppliers
Pay TV
Television Syndicators
Record Companies
Music Publishers
Book Publishers
Toy Companies
Licensing/Merchandising
Sponsors (products/services)

Above/Below the Line Budget Items

Actors
Director/Producer
Facilities
Labs
Production Houses
Video Post Production Houses
Equipment Rental Houses
Animation/Title Houses
Law Firms/Lawyers
Brokers
Accountants
Public Relations Firms
Marketing Companies/Consultants
Film Bookers
Sales Agents

Below-the-Line Deals

Below-the-line and facilities deals can also be co-production deals.
Many countries, such as Hungary, the U.S.S.R., Poland, and
Czechoslovakia, want to encourage U.S. feature production
companies to film abroad and offer below-the-line deals on crew,
studios, and equipment. However, co-production requires very
sophisticated planning and requires an experienced person who has
been there before and knows how the game is played. You can find
such people by reviewing *Variety's* list of films or *Hollywood Reporter's*
Films in Production list and learning where they were produced, then
calling the production company or producer to find out who handled
the foreign liaison and below-the-line deals.

Television Joint Ventures

European television is a relatively new frontier for feature film
financing. Both Imagine and Central TV in the U.K. have put money
in features. However, producing with foreign partners involves
numerous considerations, such as pacing, star selection, and genre,
that make many U.S. films unsuitable candidates. Foreign partners
naturally have demands on certain elements that make the films more
marketable in their markets. This should come as no surprise. They
need to take every opportunity to protect their investment.

Print and Ad Financing

One concept that has come onto the financing scene recently is the
"rent a distributor" deal. The idea is that if you **bring your picture to
a studio or distributor with a print and advertising (P&A) budget
in place**, he will more readily distribute your picture on a fee-only
basis. Since no one likes to spend money, some distributors may be
enticed by this approach, especially smaller, under-financed
companies.

Naturally, most producers want a major studio as a distributor because of its enormous clout, experience, and control of the screens. But before rushing off to finance not only production but prints and ads, the producer should examine how many films a studio can release a year.

Most studios need from 10 to 15 films per year. If they release 20 they are really doing well. Disney, Warner, and Universal need 30 films a year, so perhaps they are the more likely candidates for this kind of deal. However, even though the distributor's risk is reduced because the producer finances both the picture and the prints, it also reduces the distributor's upside. You have to ask yourself, *"With a reduced ability to earn profit will the distributor work as hard on my picture as he will when he has an investment and a greater profit potential?"*

There are three or four theatrical distributors who do *"service deals"* or *"rent-a-distributor"* deals. The deals might have an escalating fee— from 12.5 to 15 to 22 percent of gross receipts—depending on performance and whether the producer's production budget expenditures have been recouped.

The rent a distributor strategy is best utilized at certain times during the year. Christmas and Easter are not the best time since the studios' most important, high-powered pictures come out then, and every studio is competing for market share. Some studios "rent" themselves only if they get some rights participation in other media as well. If they help launch a film, they figure they are entitled to some of the gravy from the other markets. (Tough game, isn't it?)

Laboratories as Partners

Most distributors pay for P&A, but the smaller independent distributors without a healthy cash flow may not be able to, so the producer has to provide it. Or, to better their distribution deal some producers may want to provide prints for distribution. At $1,500 a print a 200-print release can cost $300,000. Or at $2,000 per print a 500-print release can cost $1 million. It's not cheap.

Investors represent only one way to raise the additional monies necessary to rent a distributor. Sometimes you can make the lab a partner by making a deal to cover print costs. The lab's investment is providing the processing and prints needed for distribution. For example, you can cut the lab in for a share in the upside profits after recoupment. Give it 25 percent of your gross receipts until the prints are paid back in full, drop it to 5 percent until the film's budget is recouped, then raise it to 10 percent thereafter. (Obviously, your other deals with investors, etc., must be written to allow you to do this should it be necessary. Bringing in a partner late in the game who gets 25 percent of the first monies affects the investors' recoupment position.) A lab deal may enable you to finance the "P" of your P&A.

The "A," or advertising portion of the P&A equation, is another area in which innovative producers can make a similar deal with a media or barter company that has lots of print and magazine ad space or television time, or both, on its hands. The company can "invest it" in a film in exchange for equity. These deals are not very common but that won't stop innovative producers from trying to put one together.

Tax-Driven Deals

There are some tax deals still remaining in Canada and Australia, but producers must comply with relatively strict production requirements on the hiring of local talent and production members. Contact the Canadian film commissions for more detailed information.

Summary

Risk capital can come from a multitude of sources. It's the producer's job to be as innovative as possible in uncovering them. Private investors, limited partnerships, letters of credit, equity investment, co-productions, joint ventures, P&A financing, and lab deals are some of the financing pieces a producer seeks out. In today's competitive financing market, pre-sales reign as one of the most viable financing elements.

GETTING
INVESTORS

GETTING INVESTORS

"A good producer keeps everyone believing."

More than the latest new camera, more than the new hi-def monitor, more than the beta-version of a graphics program, producers want to know how to raise money for their projects.

The first step is not getting the money, but **preparing a package**—a pre-production presentation—that outlines the project, cast, budget, schedule, distribution and marketing plan and predicts anticipated returns. This requires that the producer be good at writing, designing and packaging the film or video project, be enthusiastic, be thick-skinned enough for the numerous rejections he or she will encounter, have some experience in financing (or have partners who are), and some idea about where the money is and how to go about getting it.

Private Investment

Going to private investors is clearly the most expedient method for film projects if they have the ability to return the investment (and hopefully some profit). Private investment allows you much more freedom to get your film made because <u>anyone with money can help you</u>. However, distribution may still be a problem and investors will have to be convinced that distribution will be forthcoming.

Confidence

Winning over investors requires confidence and integrity. For many, this confidence comes only after they have prepared a strong package, a fabulous idea, a strong script, a great crew, superb actors, a savvy lawyer and accountant, and a distributor with experienced marketing skills. This confidence inspires confidence in others and is a critical requirement regardless of where you are looking for financial support.

The producer must also **instill confidence** in all other participants. Everyone is confident that the project is a good idea and therefore will commit to it. At precisely the right moment—not too early and not too soon, just when the alchemical cauldron begins to heat up and the package is finally ready—the producer goes out into the marketplace to secure the final ingredient: the money.

The right moment arrives when a producer can say with certainty to an investor, *"It's happening, the train is moving down the tracks, do you want to come aboard?"* He gives the investor a choice of investing. The producer makes it clear that everyone is commited to the project, that investment is really not a problem—even though it is or the producer wouldn't still be talking to investors—and that the investor is free to not invest. In the heat of the excitement, many investors surrender to the moment. The producer must then quickly close the deal.

Many producers make the mistake of asking for "help" and looking to the investor to make it all happen. *"I need you to invest, otherwise it may not happen."* No investor wants to be in this position. He wants to feel secure, and what better way to give him this feeling than by **not really needing his money.**

If you already have received a financial contribution or a distributor willing to commit marketing dollars, additional monies are much easier to raise. Your potential investors want to see that you have a distribution contract or some means to put your finished work into the marketplace to begin earning profits for them. Sophisticated investors want to be assured that you have a completion bond, which provides over-budget financing for your film if you find yourself in trouble. Your accountant's job is to provide your investors with the greatest tax advantages possible through the partnership agreements. While most tax breaks are gone, some advantages can still be structured by an experienced tax accountant. If you offer your investors a reasonable shot at profits from your movie, they may be willing to risk money they'd have to pay the tax man anyway and have some fun in the process.

Critical Mass

If you assemble your pre-production package slowly and carefully, you can achieve a *critical mass* that will improve your odds. Critical mass means you build the elements to leverage other elements. If you're a new producer it may be more difficult to get the big star first, so you get the script or film idea that begets a strong director that begets a big star. Start where you can succeed best and build from there. If you can get the big star first, that helps you leverage a director and financing. The more successful you are every step of the way, the more confident you feel and the better equipped you are to go to the next stage. Producing is taking lots of small steps—focused small steps—so at the end of your journey you have a completed film.

Keep your focus and goal clearly in front of you. Having the intelligence to separate your goals from distractions is basic. Continuing to take the right steps in an efficient and effective manner is the day-to-day work that must be done. You must have a realistic idea of how and where to start (appropriate to your station in life and what you can really do) and accurately assess your ability to inspire others. This focus and the sense that you will accomplish your goal elicits more support and agreement than anything. People want to believe, they want to be led, and **they want you to be the one to bring it all together.**

With a prepared package and your new found confidence it's time to start pitching. But not everyone is marching to the same drummer. Different people will be moved and influenced in different ways.

Right- and Left-Brain Pitches

It's important to know who your audience is when you are pitching your project, and to tailor your pitch to his or her perception. While it's never as simplistic as what I'm about to describe, this may give you some useful ideas.

Let's assume that there are basically two types of people in the world: each perceives the world very differently from the other. One type primarily uses his right brain, the other his left. (Actually, most people shift back and forth between both parts of their brains, but let me continue.) Here are some examples of the two kinds of people you will encounter during your production:

Right-Brain People
- Your *actor* is interested in the <u>emotions</u> of the character he or she is to play.
- Your *director* is interested in a compelling idea and the best way to <u>visualize</u> it.
- Your right-brained *investor* responds to the emotions, feel, look, and textural quality of your film idea.

Left-Brain People
- Your *banker* is interested in analyzing your contracts and the concrete ways in which the loan will be repaid.
- Your *left-brained investor* wants to know <u>how quickly</u> his or her money will be returned and <u>how much profit</u> the film is likely to generate over <u>what period of time</u>.

In talking with your actors, director, and composer, you will usually use evocative language because this is the mode that best suits their perceptions. You paint a picture with your words. You describe the vision for the film, its mood and tone.

When you are looking for investors, you may have to radically shift gears. Your banker and investors are not terribly keen on the mood and tone of your film. That's not what they want to hear. They want just the facts. Schedules, cash flow charts, spread sheets, market shares, and bottom lines—the very stuff that drives artistic people crazy are what they rely on in order to evaluate your project.

Different people perceive the world differently. If you want to communicate successfully with these different people, **you need to understand how they perceive the world** and to tailor your presentation appropriately. People perceive the world in a variety of primary modes, frequently switching between modes: kinetic, acoustic, visual, etc. Successful communicators are aware of the modes their audience is accessing. Successful producers are aware of the modes of perception of their investors and pitch accordingly. Film and videomakers understand their audiences modes very well and can lead them by their senses through a film experience. Clearly, this is a valuable area that requires further thought and investigation.

About Investing

Many investors will be in their left brains when they are thinking about the use of their money. One great problem with the business of raising money is that you really can't, with any sense of certainty, show your investor how and when his money will be returned. Profit is unknown. *"Well, it depends on so very many things..."* is not what your investor or banker wants to hear. It makes him real nervous.

81

Our business is very speculative, and the outcome is beyond the producer's control. *How does he or she know that the film will receive the right marketing campaign? Will the film be released at the right time? Will there be a blizzard during the opening weekend? Will we get an honest count from our distributor?* Most investors have heard about, or worse yet, gotten burnt from a movie or film deal gone bad. No wonder investors seem scarce.

The Delicate Bubble of Belief

So what do most producers do? They block such horrible thoughts from their minds to protect the sanctity of their investor's tranquility and confidence. Besides, it's far more enjoyable for the producer to use his or her story-telling skills to talk about "this wonderful film we are making." The investor is warmed from the producer's enthusiastic glow and it's hard to *"just say 'no"* If the investor looked too deeply into what could go wrong it could be depressing, and might convince him to do something else with his money. It's better for the producer to focus on the world of possibilities and happy endings.

So the dance between producer and investor begins. There are unspoken rules to be observed so that the delicate bubble of belief is not broken. The producer's job is to enthusiastically sustain the vision for what is to be. Like a magician, **he keeps everyone believing.** His vision is a dream that he's trying to make come true through the efforts of others. *"If we just keep working, and you just keep investing, we can do miraculous things!"* The more people the producer has lined up, the more real it begins to look to everyone, and the more real the vision actually becomes. The producer's art is a kind of alchemy. He mixes in enthusiasm, talent, and money, and voilà!—a film emerges from the smoke and mirrors.

Misadventures in Hollywood

When I was 26, I obtained the rights to a best-selling novel and just enough development money from United Arts Theaters to get something going. But I didn't have enough experience. What the executives at United Artists wanted to find out was whether I could, using their name, their 1,200 theaters, and a little money, leverage the balance of the financing. I didn't.

I spent a year-and- a-half pitching the project and got into most of the studios, but didn't know how to use the leverage I had. In fact, I didn't know I had any leverage! I was so focused on directing that I could think of little else. I would have had a much easier time getting the film made if I had taken an associate producer credit (and role) and brought in those who knew how to play the financing game, but I was afraid to let others participate for fear of losing what little control I thought I had. When the option expired, I was too tired and too broke to renew it.

The lesson I learned was: **you work with what you have and what you don't have you get,** which may mean letting others support the project. I had enough chutzpah to acquire the rights to a best–selling book but not enough experience to cast myself correctly. I held out for something that I couldn't get. My friends could commiserate with me on how the *"studios just didn't have the vision..."* but that wasn't the same as having the satisfaction of producing something.

The world was hungry for new material and I was able to get my foot in most doors, but I didn't know when to get out of my own way. I could have used the rejections I was receiving along the way as lessons and modified my behavior and expectations. When you are packaging a project, the job is to get the best people for the job (even if that means not hiring yourself!).

83

A worthy package stands a good chance of attracting financing, although it may take a year or two. It's not unusual for producers to spend many years trying to get a movie off the ground, and it's not a good idea to start the financing search before you are ready. But once you are ready, you must use all your resources to move quickly because your own energy may not last forever. If you don't get your film or video financed after a certain period of time, you get frustrated, bitter, and tired. So when your package is finally set, contact everyone you know and start pulling the financing together.

Video Financing: The Three Strike Rule

I've developed and produced enough video projects to know where to go to find financing and distribution, and over the last few years have developed my own "three-strike rule." Generally speaking, if after three pitches to buyers I know there is still no deal, I move on. If the project is rejected by three of the most likely buyers, then the marketplace is telling me *"no thanks."* Sometimes the project is resurrected later in another form, sometimes not.

Videos have a shorter gestation rate than films. They are quicker to develop, cost far less to produce, are made faster than movies, and get into the marketplace and begin earning revenues sooner. The financing arc on a feature may take years, on a video only months. If you are like me, and desire instant gratification, videos will suit you.

I like videos because, at any one time, I can have a dozen in development, a handful in production, and many more in release. Features move forward very slowly (or not at all), although the financial rewards can be much greater.

End Users as Financiers

Conventional wisdom suggests it's more advantageous to get financing from an end user, whether it's a broadcaster, home video company, or theatrical distributor. The thinking goes that if the end user invests in the film or video he is motivated to get his money back by making sure the product is successfully distributed. His self-interest serves your interests. If your financing doesn't come from an end user you must rely on other resources.

A second argument frequently made for going to end users for financing is that it's usually easier. An end user understands movie and video deals. It doesn't matter if your end-user investment partner is domestic or foreign because he will protect his downside, either through his own distribution efforts, or by selling it to others. European broadcasters and distributors, for example, carry the new checkbooks today. They want to finance pictures in the $12 to $15 million range that have recognizable casts and successful genres. (Who doesn't? That's half the cost of a studio picture.)

Private Investors

Another school of thought suggests that non-industry financing, the private investor route, is best because the investor is less sophisticated and makes fewer demands about the kind of film or video produced.

Many, many films have been financed by private investors. Now, however, savvy private investors are staying away from films because they know the heyday of pre-selling is gone. It used to be that when a film was pre-sold the investor could see a pretty decent rate of return as a result of the once-burgeoning video rental-store business. Today the competition to sell to the video rental market is greater because a retailer no longer buys most "B" titles but prefers "A's," which are almost solely produced by the studios. Video-rental stores don't want hard-to-market "B" films when they can have "A" pictures (for the

85

same price) that bring greater visibility and higher rentals. For an investor in independent "B" films today, the risk is heightened and the rate of return diminished. Why shouldn't he look for other kinds of investments?

What Investors Want

When I first started raising money for very low-budget films and documentaries, I was very surprised by what some investors wanted. It had little or nothing to do with their money and their actual investment—they really didn't care whether their money was returned or not. **They were interested in what the film had to say and getting a message out**. And some were just interested in being around film makers.

Unsophisticated investors (meaning those that haven't invested in films or videos before) go through your prospectus, listen to your presentation, and scrutinize you very carefully. They ask many questions that you must be prepared to answer. They will certainly have questions, which they won't ask, that you will need to answer. Here are some things they like and need to hear:

> 1. The film (or video) **will make a lot of money**, more than their combined investments, and maybe a whole lot more than that. (How can you demonstrate this?)

> 2. There will be a large publicity campaign that will **generate enormous public excitement** and awareness, and lots of people will want to see the film or video they've been hearing about. (How can you demonstrate this?)

> 3. Your film is a class act with high-profile elements. There are **well-known**, prestigious stars, directors and/or writers in your film. Your film is based on a **best-selling** book, a life story, a high-profile news event, or a literary masterpiece.

4. Your film will be shot on **exquisite locations,** or will be loaded with special effects, or will have some visual element that is really terrific, or all of the above.

5. They can participate or **get involved** at some level. Can they visit the set, go to parties, go to the premiere, meet the actors?

6. **They have a choice** about investing in your film or not investing in it. They don't want to feel pressured, or coerced, or that the film's future depends on their money. This puts way too much pressure and responsibility on the investors. It's the producer's job to get the film made.

Some Other Thoughts

1. **Money attracts money.** If you already have some money in your project it will bring a sigh of relief to your investors. No one wants to be first (unless there is some financial reward for doing so), and by sharing the risk with other investors, everyone's comfort level rises.

If you have done your homework and put together an admirable package and an honest agreement, you will find investors. If your project has integrity and if you are offering a fair deal to investors, you already stand head and shoulders above the crowd of other producers beating on the same doors. Honesty is very attractive to investors, and they know it when they see it.

2. There will be lots of films that look better than yours because they have bigger budgets, but **that doesn't mean they are better.** Investors also recognize good films. An example is SEX, LIES AND VIDEOTAPE, a good film that cost a fraction of what the average studio spends on catering per year.

Don't confuse money with quality. **A good film is competitive in the marketplace** because the audience for good films is growing. Tastes are changing, movie audiences are getting older, and they are demanding more from movies. They want better, more intelligent stories, finer acting, and movies that bring some meaning into their lives.

Independents have one significant advantage over the studios: they can make good films for little money. This is attractive to investors because there is tremendous upside in producing quality films within reasonable budgets. Independents know that the limited money they are able to raise must go into the film and be seen on the screen. The fewer fees taken out of the budget, the better the investment package appears to investors. No investor likes to see a producer paying himself large fees from the budget; no investor wants to fall victim to a "hit and run" producer. If you make quality films or videos, you will find quality investors.

3. When you want a hundred people to show up at a party you invite a hundred and thirty. When you line up your investors you need to do the same thing because some may fall through and not deliver on their pledges. Some will have "cash flow" or "stock market" or "personal problems" by the time you return to get the check. **Have commitments for more money than you actually need.** It does wonders for your self esteem and attracts even more investors. **People run to abundance and run from scarcity.** If you have more money than you need, you build leverage in your distribution negotiations and you won't have to cave in on deal points. If you don't have all the money you need, the distributor's money does the talking and you lose your negotiating strength. If you don't need the money you can make tougher deals, which benefits your investors.

4. Financing is networking. Whether investors say "yes" or "no" to your project, be sure to get other names and contacts from them. If they say "yes" they'll be inclined to think of others who might like to

invest. If they say "no," they may feel guilty and at least will want to give you something for free—like someone else's name. Fine. **You can use every contact you can get.**

5. Make sure your lawyer complies with all state laws and SEC regulations in preparing your investment documents. If you proceed in an unprofessional, haphazard manner you can be shut down and suffer terrible consequences. For example, you are not allowed to advertise your project in newspapers or magazines. In some cases you must qualify your investors—they must be able to afford the risk—and they may be required to have earned over $250,000 per year for the last several years. Discuss this with your attorney to learn whether he or she must qualify every potential investor.

The regulations become complex and usually very expensive if you try to make a public offering. Low-budget filmmakers are better off putting the money on the screen and not into the cost of a public offering. Public offerings are best when you are financing a package of films.

Summary

The producer lives, dreams and works in the world of *"yes, it can happen"*. Every step is a focused, highly intended move toward the premiere. The producer is amassing support with every waking hour. The producer believes. Everyone else believes. Even the money eventually falls into place.

Attitude and preparation are everything. Knowing what to do first is important. Build critical mass. Know the appropriate manner in which to communicate to your creative staff, and your financial supporters. Knowing what they want and need will give you the ability to answer their questions with clarity and confidence. As you build your creative and financial base your confidence will grow. Your enthusiasm will mount and you'll soon be into production.

PRE-SALES

PRE-SALES

"Foreign pre-sale monies can make up 40% to 60% of the budget."

Introduction to Pre-sales

Years ago, your sales agent could pre-sell a film to foreign and domestic markets for more than 100 percent of the production budget. Experienced producers were in profits even before the films were made. But those days are virtually gone (with the exception of "franchise sequels" like the RAMBOs or NIGHTMARE ON ELM STREETs or virtually anything with Arnold) because there were too many pre-sold films that performed poorly. Now—just to get their films made—producers scramble to make up their entire production budget from a combination of pre-sale sources.

Pre-selling is costly because you can forfeit as much as 50 percent when the sales agent's fee is added to the foreign distributor's share. Any overages (monies received beyond the pre-sell advance or guarantee) are filtered through the local distributor and the sales agent back to you. There are fees and costs at the local level; there is the sales agent's fee. That's why producers don't see much, if anything, coming back beyond the advance.

In most territories the local distributor charges fees similar to those a major charges here—anything from 30 to 50 percent. The foreign home video royalty is about 20 percent. This royalty goes into the same pot as the theatrical revenues, and then the sales agent takes a fee.

However, foreign pre-sale monies are important because they can make up 40, 50, or 60 percent of the budget. Co-productions and pre-buys now account in large part for many films in the $3 million or less category. However, most distributors feel that a picture costing less than $5 million won't have enough international box office draw.

Pre-sales are made through sales agents working with international distribution companies. There are about 40 countries that distribute American films. Each has about 3 distributors. Eight of these countries (the U.K., Japan, Germany, France, Italy, Australia, Spain, and Scandinavia) make up 85 percent of American foreign film sales (video and TV included). Some are not well financed and some can deliver up-front guarantees. What you need to do is find a reputable sales agent.

When your sales agent pre-sells your film, you do not get cash but a letter of credit that you take to your bank. The bank loans you the money using the letter of credit as collateral. This arrangement works only if you deal with a reputable firm known by your bank, which is willing to loan against their paper. A pre-sale agreement greatly comforts your equity partners because they know that sales and distribution are in place. Fees range from 7.5 to 10 to 15 percent without guarantees. With guarantees, the sales agent fee is from 17.5 to 20 to 35 percent, depending on whether the sales agent is trying to get cash or a deal in place.

It's very difficult for independents to do pre-sales without expertise. Alliances are critical. How do you identify a good rep? Longevity. Ask around. (See the sales reps list in the Appendix.)

In order to make successful pre-sales, common wisdom says you need an "A" movie, with a great script, director, and cast. On an "A" picture, from 50 to 75 percent of the budget is covered from foreign sales. On a low budget film, 75 percent of the budget can be covered. Each territory must be analyzed for each picture. The growth areas are in television and not, as they formerly were, in video. The stronger the ancillary markets, the harder it is to segregate or splinter the rights. Distributors want to participate at every level.

Street Gossip

Some pre-sale street gossip (although this may change by the time you read it):

England. The AMC chain has revamped its theaters. Theatrical business is healthier than ever before. There is good business in home video and the new satellites (SKY and BSB) will create demand for more product.

France is dead.

Japan is picky. They will pay high prices for foreign films but very few indie films are bought for Japan. They will only do all rights deals. Action/adventure with violence is king. No comedies.

Australia. The big American pictures do best. Price ceiling fixing is not illegal so everyone gets the same low prices. They limit the up-front guarantees but do give a back-end should the film perform well theatrically.

Italy tv price has ceilings. Action/adventure with violence is king.

Latin America is less important. Comedies OK.

Germany. Only the big films work. Video is soft. There are too many retailers. German TV pays less than Spain, France, or the U.K. now. Action/adventure with violence is king.

The American Film Market (AFM) in Los Angeles is taking a leadership role to help in co-productions and joint ventures and is a source for what works and what doesn't.

95

The Value of Genre

The amount of money that you get on foreign pre-sales is dependent on the genre, or kind of film, that you produce. A low-budget (sans stars) comedy with a lot of American humor isn't going to get much from the foreign market in pre-sales. An action picture tends to play very well across all markets and can generate anywhere from 40 to 50 or even 60 percent of budget.

Horror is difficult. It's very strong in some markets and weak in others because of heavy censorship. Financially, horror is safer than a domestic comedy.

Drama isn't as strong as horror or action but probably is more valuable than comedy.

Art films have a life of their own and live or die by critical reviews on a territory-by-territory basis. Art films are nearly impossible to pre-sell until they've been completed and screened.

An English-language parlor drama may sell well in Europe but be hard to distribute in the U.S. The question is whether you are producing American art and trying to go overseas, or the reverse.

The Pre-Sale

Most producers look to a sales agent to make foreign sales on his or her behalf. The best time for a producer to call on foreign sales agents is when the packaging process has been completed, the final script is drafted, a confirmed (or nearly confirmed and committed) cast list is ready, and a production company of repute is in place with its key production figures, such as director, director of photography, and set designer. The sales agent won't have anything to sell unless the project is viable. The producer can help a sales agent enormously by providing not only a very strong package but art work and graphics that demonstrate to the sales agent's buyers the ease of marketing and the high profitability of the film.

FOREIGN PRE-SALES: RICHARD LORBER INTERVIEW

An understanding of how the pre-sale market works comes best from Richard Lorber, co-founder of Fox/Lorber, a foreign sales agent, who frequently travels to the foreign markets to make pre-sales and distribution arrangements for his producer clients.

How does someone approach you and become your client?

"Many of the people we deal with are first-time something-or-others, whether it's first-time producer or first-time director—and those are the people most often breaking into the low-budget film production realm. We need to know that they've really done a fairly thorough job lining up their ducks and handling these things as professionally as possible. Since we are not in the development business, it's not of interest to us when someone brings an idea for a script. We can't get a script financed."

What are the budget ranges you deal in on independent projects?

"Most of the things we've dealt with have been in the low-budget range, from $500,000—often the range of truly made-for-home-video productions—to about $4.5 million. We're currently handling projects at both ends of that spectrum and a couple in between. A couple of years ago the low-budget projects were more genre-oriented to exploit the then still solvent video industry, which was still echoing from the boom years. Now the echo is inaudible. The projects we're getting are <u>not</u> in the horror, T&A, or teen comedy genre vein aimed toward the worldwide home video market, but are more quality-oriented visions that are modeled on the Jarmusch,

Soderbergh models of independent, quality, and conceptually interesting films with strong scripts: It's the John Sayles model—in which the film really has a shot at some interesting niche theatrical-release potential."

Does that mean that there is finally an expanding international market for tasteful film?

"Not exactly. In a nutshell, it's just as hard to sell crap as it is to sell quality. But now all the incentives have gone out of pushing genre junk. The worldwide video market has cooled off to the point that there's no room on the shelf anymore for that stuff. Therefore, those of us who really believe in quality and like it (but from time to time get tempted by the easy buck of a quick genre film) now can feel more morally pure about the fact that we can put our energies into stuff we really believe in. It's all hard to sell. But if you've got a good script. . ."

If an independent filmmaker wanted to thoughtfully and strategically consider making a type of film, what kind of film might find the most success?

"The model is invariably the most recent successful independent film. We're a lot different than most companies in that we're broadly diversified but focused in our selection of product. We're very selective in trying to find product that we feel strategically can work in a lot of different media and markets. We won't take something on only because it's going to have foreign potential. We'll look at something that we think also has some domestic potential. We look at it from the point of view of a rep, who might actually wind up selling it to a company that's in the international distribution and sales business—a company that may very well be a competitor of ours. We'll also look at it directly as a sales agent and distributor, where we might sell on a pre-sale basis to a particular buyer in a particular territory or group of territories for pre-sale."

Recently I've heard a lot about the downturn in independent production. What's your experience been?

"It's hard for me to be too specific. There are some companies in the U.K. right now that are concerned with the downturn in production. Production is down possibly as much as 35 percent in 1990 from 1989, and the year before was down substantially from the previous year. So the companies that have built their business in distribution in particular territories are finding a shortage of product, particularly with the demise of many independent film production and theatrical distribution companies in the U.S. and elsewhere.

"Therefore, a particular distributor in a particular territory realizes that he not only has to worry about getting the rights to his territory, but about making sure there's adequate product flow. Therefore he may be more inclined to take an equity interest and put money on the table to help a producer get the film made, rather than simply worrying about getting the best possible deal for his own territory. That's beginning to happen more and more in the U.K. and in other territories where established companies have just run out of product.

"It makes good financial sense because invariably the distributors get a better deal in terms of license fees for their own territories. They avoid having to bid competitively for a finished film and are basically pre-buying something with a good equity share. The problem is whether they can recoup in a meaningful way through the equity investment. In some cases they're not worried about it because they can recoup it on an all-rights buy-out basis from their own territories.

"Or, they may also broaden their distribution rights to become a principal distributor in, say, the U.K., and also be the sales agent for all of Europe. With Europe moving toward 1992, there is more and more intra-European dealing going on among companies in different countries that are also becoming co-production partners to the exclusion of the U.S. as the main partner."

This would indicate that producers should pay a lot of attention to the European markets on both the sales and co-production levels. Yes?

"New producers should look for European partners who can work on a lot of different levels. They should ask themselves, 'Who is a European partner and a strong distributor in a specific media in my own territory? Who is a distributor with an output deal with one of the major television networks who can guarantee me up-front fees on television as well as theatrical and video? Who is a distributor with an interest in broadening his distribution base into a sales agent role in other territories, or who has an alliance with a sales agent who can guarantee buying foreign rights? In addition, is there an investor looking at an equity participation for whatever value, and can this be tax exempt or sheltered?' It's very important that the independent producer research the profile of the particular prospects in different markets and adapt his presentation to their needs and capabilities, or find a representative who can do it."

Most producers are too busy trying to package their films. How do they learn about the foreign markets?

"Independent producers can learn a great deal, surprisingly, in a conversation over a drink in the Majestic Bar at the Cannes festival. And it's important for producers to get out of the film ghetto a bit. But I think it's a waste of time for the independent producer to go to the Cannes Film Festival. It's much more important for him to go to a MIP or MIPCOM television festival, in a businesslike setting where he will see people he knows in the film business operating in another market, in other media. I'm not saying that the festival circuits are not beneficial, but an independent producer lured to Cannes by industry razzle-dazzle can get caught up in it without analyzing or perhaps

100

without being able to analyze where the money is flowing and how the deals are being structured. Television is the fastest growing segment of the international entertainment market right now and is probably the place for an independent producer to start.

"These days Europe and Japan are good places for TV sales and features. Pre-sales and equity deals provide up-front financing. New foreign markets are opening up because the value of the dollar is low and because U.S. movies are perceived as good investments."

I know a lot of producers get themselves to the festivals or markets and then find themselves watching their colleagues' movies rather than getting themselves out there to learn the business.

"It's important for film producers to see how theatrical features are being sold in the television marketplace and where the larger share of the money is coming from these days, rather than in the video marketplace, which is basically flat. If a film producer had three markets he had to go to as part of his educational process, I advise him not go to the Cannes festival if that means missing out on American Film Market (AFM). In addition to AFM, I advise going to one or two of the television markets, or a television market and one combining video and television."

What's your perception of the differences in these markets?

"AFM is good because it is an American market and producers will have a high degree of exchange with American companies. Product quality tends to be a little better at AFM than at MIFED, MIP, or MIPCOM. This is important because it's the main international television market.

"MIP is the primary and long-established television market, still somewhat dominated by the majors, studios, and big networks.

"MIPCOM is a smaller market, and was conceived as a television and multimedia (meaning television and video) market incorporating the newer satellite and cable technologies. It draws on a wider, more diverse array of entrepreneurs and on representatives of other media. It is faster growing, more interesting, and probably more productive for an independent.

"The Video Software Dealers Association (VSDA) is meaningless for producers because it's for distributors who sell to video stores. The Cannes festival is too distracting. Producers will learn more by attending AFM or MIPCOM and then a quality international film festival like the Berlin Film Festival or the Venice, London, Telluride, or U.S. film festivals, where they can meet distributors, reps, and people on a more relaxed basis. These festivals allow producers to get to know people outside the market setting, in which people are pressed, harried, and there to make sales. What I am saying is that you must "network!" You can't do this sitting in Iowa reading Michael Wiese's books.

"Strategically speaking, it's even better if the producers can wangle an invitation to be on a panel, or be a festival speaker, or have a short film, documentary, or some other piece of work exhibited that attracts distributor attention."

You're very creative when it comes to pulling money together. Say you make a pre-sale that's really just a contract. How do you convert that to cash for your production?

"Pre-sales to Japan or Europe sometimes get you money. You might get a cash float or negotiate an arrangement alongside the guarantee in which the buyer also provides resources from his bank (foreign or domestic) to your cash flow. If you go to a company that's strong—a

Mitsubishi or a JVC in Japan, let's say—obviously part of the deal is that you need more than a contract for negative pickup or pre-buy. You need to cash flow it. They may be interested in helping you do that, and may take a commission on it.

"Companies pre-buying packages at a significant level are known to the big financial institutions and can provide either a letter of credit, which is almost as good as cash and can be borrowed against, or actually provide the cash. They may say 'We don't need a letter of credit,' a position that Vestron used to take. In some cases they help arrange financing of their guarantee, which MCEG has recently done. MCEG set up what was basically a banking division to help producers finance and cash flow their paper contracts.

"Contracts are effectively collateralized contracts. The contract becomes collateral for a loan."

This is all very heavy duty for most producers starting out. How can a producer create leverage so that he'll be able to get financing?

"Presumably producers have made something before—one or two shorts, documentaries, TV commercials, music video clips, or a TV series. It's almost unprecedented for a first-time director to get an independent feature financed without any previous work on the screen, unless a package is put together with so many other partners that his credibility is not in question.

"If a producer can say, "Look, we've raised half a million dollars from RCA and we're looking for a million for your territory," that will definitely help. What most enhances credibility, and what is the most difficult to get, is a commitment from a major U.S. theatrical distributor. Sometimes a foreign investor is an asset in linking up with a U.S. company. A U.K. or Japanese company that gets excited about

103

a project may say, 'We want to do this, so maybe we can help by introducing you to a company in the U.S. that we work with a lot."

"In some cases an individual buyer in a territory helps an independent producer by bringing him a sales agent from, say, the U.K., who might be interested in taking up the rest of the territories because the buyer has bought from him before. So the U.K. guy says, 'This is great. I can only commit for the U.K., but let me call up XYZ international sales agents, who may be interested in making a guarantee for the rest of the world that gives you what you need.' "

The foreign markets may be just too much for a first-timer to take on. What are the opportunities in the U.S.?

"One strong area of opportunity is cable. All of the cable networks are getting involved in original production. HBO, of course, has been financing features for probably the last 5 or 7 years. Showtime recently announced Showtime Pictures, which is now actively soliciting projects. They finance the entire budget and retain all rights with the provision that there will be no U.S. theatrical release prior to a premiere on their cable TV network. Showtime pictures are in the $3- to $5-million range. Showtime is eager for any theatrical exposure in which they retain the rights and market the film through Viacom, in order to enhance the value in ancillary media. A producer has to decide at the outset if making a fully-financed film that has no exposure and will not be released theatrically in its primary market is too bitter a pill to swallow.

"Other basic cable networks with advertisers such as USA Network make films in the $1- to $2-million range. Even Lifetime, and certainly Turner, is in the feature film business, not financing the entire negative costs perhaps, but financing half or more. Turner is involved in so many different areas in the feature business that it's hard to know exactly where he puts his money."

Any other stones a producer shouldn't fail to turn over?

"The key is to pay attention to the evolving technologies and see whether any of them want to build assets in the form of ownership of copyrights where they might finance production, which is frequently the case. It's notably been the case with the satellite networks launched out of the U.K. It's been the case with U.S. networks that are beginning to move toward national distribution, the expectation being ownership of their productions. All the U.S. networks have formed international entrepreneurial units to invest in, and in some cases fully finance, international co-productions. At varying times all the networks have been involved in financing feature films. That's going to increase as the networks are deregulated."

Producers need to get inside the heads of the network program buyers. Why do broadcasters want to produce their own films?

"They want to build a proprietary base of programming. The goal is not so much to own a library as to have films they control totally and can promote heavily, films not available to their competitors. It's worked for the networks—that's the basis of the made-for-television movie. We see so few theatrical films on the networks because of the made-for-television movie. The networks prefer to make their own movies, movies that cannot be shown on pay TV or basic cable, and cannot be released on home video until the network is ready to do so. Another advantage to the networks in financing their own productions is that these films can be designed around the interests of their most desirable audiences."

Let's discuss the various genres of films. What is the dominant genre for pre-sales?

"The dominant genre is still the action movie. World audiences like action, suspense, thrillers, and dramas that have the typical elements

105

of fast pacing, fast cars, fast men, fast women, and guns and
helicopters with occasional explosions but not excessive graphic
violence. They aim for speed, action, suspense, and thrills. Similarly,
the science fiction genre is preferable to the horror genre, the
thriller/suspense/mystery genre to the slasher genre. The straight
horror genre has largely fallen out of favor except for those with
superb special effects in a non-slasher context or with a
fantasy–science fiction aspect.

"Horror-fantasy films are important, but to an extent the established
franchises—FRIDAY THE THIRTEENTH, NIGHTMARE ON
ELM STREET—perform less and less well. I think it would be
difficult today to establish such unending-sequel franchises in those
genres. A LETHAL WEAPON–type genre franchise would be easier
to establish than a NIGHTMARE ON ELM STREET one because
the horror market, whose growth was fueled by the expansion of
home video, has fallen out of favor with home video's decline. All the
horror films anyone will ever want to see are already on the video
shelves.

"The most desirable films are those having a broad appeal and genre
elements that are not extreme. The genre elements that work are the
gut-wrenching aspects of a thriller, the scary elements (but not the
explicit gore) of a horror film, and the erotic elements (but not the
explicit sexuality) of a T&A movie.

"More and more international buyers scratch their heads and avoid
giving you a specific genre when you ask what kind of movies work in
their markets. They say, 'I don't know; just give me a real movie,'
which ultimately means a movie that compels my interest, doesn't
insult me, has a good script, good characters, good pacing, and is
something I care about. Buyers have also turned away from the made-
for-TV movies that have dominated U.S. networks because they're
tired of the disease-of-the-week topicality of American network
movies. This works very well on American networks but doesn't

appeal to a broad enough audience, even though production values are high."

Earlier we spoke about high quality, low budget independent films. How do they work in the international pre-sale market?

"SEX, LIES AND VIDEOTAPE will play all over the world because it's a very good movie with an excellent script, superb performances, and some cast and marquee value. James Spader and Andie MacDowell already had careers—perhaps not big careers, but they're not anonymous, either. More importantly, SEX has genre elements: suspense, eroticism, wit and humor, and a contemporaneousness that works well. It won't be as big as a LETHAL WEAPON or RAMBO, but within a niche (the low-budget independent American picture niche) it will do much better than anything else in that niche. And it will benefit by virtue of the fact that it's had superb reviews and won some awards."

What about Spike Lee's work? Does it travel?

"My comments about SEX apply to a much lesser extent to Spike Lee movies. That's because he is so genre-specific. Irrespective of what you think of his films, because they come out of a black context they are seen as a particularly American problem that doesn't translate well overseas. There is a curiosity about it, but many international buyers look at a film dealing specifically with the race problem in America as America's problem. They are interested for other reasons and buy the film on the basis of its intrinsic humor, wit, character roles, and excitement, not because of its American racial subject matter."

Let's say a producer wants to sell his work to domestic television. Where would you recommend he go?

"I don't recommend the big agencies like William Morris. It's not that I have anything against William Morris; it's because high-powered talent agencies are not equipped to serve the financing needs of the independent producer, although they can help later on when it's a question of attracting talent to a project that already has distribution attached. While a big agency is not the first step, you could talk to a friendly agent for advice and to identify the best reps or distributors to use. It's been my experience that agents are best when the deals come to them rather than their actually having to go out and hit the bushes. It's very hard work."

You'd recommend then that the agent be used to help package the talent?

"The value of the agent is to be supportive of the picture to the point where he'll write you a letter that says, 'I've submitted a script to DeNiro and he has, based on my recommendation and his own view of the script, indicated his interest. Subject to availability and financial considerations, he might be interested in being involved in it.' That letter can be a very powerful tool in the hands of the film rep or distributor who's trying to raise the money and pre-sell the film. The agent is not going to be the one who goes out and raises the money."

Actors aren't as difficult to get as most producers assume?

"Exactly. Obviously, it depends whether you're dealing with talent in the six-figure range or talent in the seven-figure range. Remember, with the downturn in production there are a surprisingly large number of actors and actresses who are looking for work, and they'd rather take less of a fee for a film they really believe in and feel will be an enhancement to their career than for a film that is purely a commercial undertaking and not something they're going to be proud of. There are also other ways of getting talent involved, which involve equity interest in the film and various other things.

"Using a major agent from a talent agency is where you begin. Going the route of finding a film rep or a distributor is more meaningful when it comes to putting the financing together."

108

There is so much that producers need to know. They need a foreign sales rep who understands the intricacies of the territories to cut through all the noise. They need a talent agent to complete their package. You could spend years barking up the wrong tree.

"That's the point. If a producer really wants to learn the business to the point that he becomes a film rep or a distributor, or both, then he should try to do it all himself. But the best strategy for a producer is to learn the ins and outs and to be able to **help plan with the film rep** or distributor. The producer should be worrying about other things.

"If the relationship is as it should be, the sales agent feeds information to the producer, which gives him ammunition that in turn helps the sales agent and distributor sell the picture. The sales agent's information can involve additional cast commitments or clarifications of cast roles. It can involve sites and locations. It can involve producing the film under the treaties of countries with tax benefits or other financial advantages, as in Canada (where a majority of Canadian cast elements and crew creates much higher value in certain territories). That is the kind of information the sales agent should be bouncing to the producer. The producer should be trying to solve these problems if the solutions will help the sales agent get the deal financed."

Upside/Downside

There are lots of places in the world for your foreign sales rep to go for pre-sales. The people he goes to will play down the value of your product because they don't want to pay for it. If you do make a pre-sale you give up the upside. You get your money, which gets your film made, which is what you want to do. But in getting the pre-sale money you lock yourself into an agreement that limits your returns should the film perform exceptionally well. It's one of the necessary evils inherent in the pre-sale. If you wait until the film is finished before selling it (and your picture is very good), you'll make better deals. But if you shop a finished film too long, buyers may think there is something wrong with it and you can get a worse deal. Timing and creating a high perception of your film are very, very important at any stage in the sales game.

If you can appear to be fully financed (so you seem not to need anyone's money) and go into production (and perhaps have a little something to show that is great) and then go out to pre-sale, you may be in the best of all positions. You don't know yet whether your picture will be great, but you have something great to show. And your sales agent may be able to generate a bidding war before your film is finished.

The upside comes when you have a big, big hit. This will increase your revenues in all markets. If you've pre-sold those markets, you've probably lost the upside.

You do pre-sales for one of two main reasons. Either you don't believe in the upside of your picture or you simply need the money to cover your budget.

STRATEGIES FOR FOREIGN SALES

In the foreign market, directors are of great concern to buyers. Cast is also important and elevates the status of a genre movie. Name actors can be hired to do cameos for two or three days, which gives you the added marque value you need but keeps the budget down. The sales rep can help you make sure the names you plan to use mean something worldwide.

Some argue that you need a major U.S. release before there is any significant sales interest overseas. Five years ago, sales could be made on films without a U.S. theatrical window. That's less true today, by most accounts. HBO's films with $3 million budgets couldn't do it. In the U.K., for example, there are 1,400 screens, with 450 U.S. films and another 200 to 250 films— totaling from 600 to 700 films— competing for these screens in one year. But it really comes down to a matter of degree and quality. Films are being made in every budget category. If they are good, some films transcend their inherent budgetary limitations and perform well in the marketplace. But this doesn't happen very often. Any film that gets completed will be looked at. It's much harder to sell an unfinished film with a low budget.

NEGATIVE PICKUPS

Negative pickups are a guarantee by a studio or a distributor, that they will pay a specific amount when the producer delivers the finished film. There are certain conditions the producer must meet. For example, the film cannot deviate significantly from the script that was approved by the distributor. Negative pickups usually go to producers who have a track record with studios and distributors. Negative pickups occur once a film is finished and the distributor evaluates the film. The risk of financing a film without a distributor is high, but if the producer creates an appealing picture the reward may be great. However financing may be extremely difficult because without a distribution contract or negative pickup guarantee to take to the bank, investors will be wary.

A negative pickup is a coup for a producer because it means he or she can go straight to the bank for financing. Distribution is assured from the outset. A negative pick-up proves that the distributor is serious about the film and will go to the marketing efforts of at least recouping their money. Investors are happy because it lessens their risk.

Distributors know good packages are shopped and eventually picked up. That's good for the producer because it puts doubt in the distributor's mind, making him prey to the thought that if he doesn't buy the film now, his competition will. And it's always cheaper for the distributor to buy a film before completion than after, when he might have to participate in a bidding war.

A negative pickup is hard to get but can be one of the best ways to finance your film because it locks in distribution, removes some risk from your investors, and assures domestic distribution, which is of enormous importance in securing foreign and ancillary sales.

VALUE OF DOMESTIC DISTRIBUTION

Successful domestic distribution for independent films can be difficult to obtain on any scale. Domestic distribution is, however, very important because all ancillary sales revenues will be a result of how the film performed in the U.S. The promotion, the reviews, and word of mouth brings significant value to television and home video venues, here and abroad.

Many producers are happy if they recoup a large part of production costs and all theatrical advertising are from theatrical revenues. On THE BEACH BOYS film (which I executive-produced for Vestron), we were happy to recoup only advertising and release costs from the film's brief theatrical exposure. The production costs and profits came from all video and television sales worldwide. Without a domestic release, it's tough to get the economics to work since everything is tied to the U.S. performance. Besides, investors may shy away from a project that doesn't have distribution in place. *"How are you going to get my money back?"* they'll ask.

A foreign sales agent is needed for foreign sales. On the domestic side a producer ought to do it himself. There are only a few independent distributors to visit and he can easily access them. You will already have legal fees so why add sales agent's fees to the domestic sale? As for the studios, it's fairly certain that a major isn't going to get involved with any sort of pre-sale for a small independent film. Although once in a while, the rules are broken, as in the negative pickup of STAND AND DELIVER.

The standard domestic theatrical deal with small independent companies these days is a P&A commitment with little or no advance and usually includes all domestic rights.

The best shot at getting rights pre-sold domestically is to look to major television programmers like HBO (which would be interested in a combination of video and pay-TV rights) or SHOWTIME (which also would be interested in a bundle of rights—pay and syndication) that doesn't include theatrical.

Domestic distribution means the film can either be packaged for mass audience success (big stars, director, genre) and sold on the appeal of its packaged elements before it is actually produced, or it can be a small, independent film that relies on a good script, a good director, and good actors that probably won't be sold to distribution until someone can see how good it is. This means the film must be produced and paid for up front, which is very risky for any investor even though he believes in the filmmaker heart and soul. But if the film is really terrific, there is enormous upside because the filmmaker can strike a better deal and retain a greater profit share than would have been possible in a pre-sale deal.

DISTRIBUTORS AND DISTRIBUTION

One of the biggest elements in your financial package is a distributor. Finding one is a strategic art unto itself. All distributors are different, and the producer must ferret out the one best suited to the film he is producing. The producer must learn from distributors and other producers the reputation and marketing abilities of potential distributors—not through rumors, but from relayed first-hand experiences with these companies. He must look at films recently distributed by these companies and understand why they release and advertise them as they do. There are fewer and fewer distributors for independent films, so this research is very important.

Distribution is the centerpiece of financing. If your distribution contract (and cash flow to you) doesn't work, the entire business plan falls apart. That's why it's extremely important to have a highly experienced lawyer worry over the incongruities of your distribution contracts and negotiate your deal. Ideally, he's already negotiated many contracts with the very same distributor in the past and knows the contract through and through.

The problem is that your distributors will **interpret** the distribution contract and how cash should paid to you before it is sent. **They do the math.** You cash the check (if any).

There are a variety of places where the accounting can go askew. The theatrical exhibitor takes in cash at the box office and, naturally, interprets his deal with the distributor using his own self-interest as guide. The distributor will naturally make the toughest deal he can with the exhibitor and enforce collection. The distributor, having just gone through enormous hassle and inconvenience to collect his share of the box office take, is not in a generous mood when interpreting how much money goes to the producer. The distributor will use his own best "judgment" and interpretation of the distribution contract in writing the smallest check possible (if any). The problem with distribution is the nature of the trickle-down cash flow, which encounters numerous interruptions on its way to the producer. These dynamics also occur in home video distribution. (See Wiese's <u>Home Video: Producing for the Home Market</u>, and <u>Film & Video Marketing</u> for more detailed information on distribution deals.)

The distribution contract significantly affects the financing of your film or video. I've always thought the best deal would be for the distributor, the producer, and the investors to stand under the "money

waterfall" at the same time, sharing in profits once their costs were recouped. In my ideal world where everyone shares the same ideas of fairness, the distributor would take a small distribution fee (say 15 percent) and recoup print and advertising costs. Then the production budget would be recouped. Then the distributor, investor, and producer would share through some equitable formula. Simple and elegant.

But it doesn't work. Why? Because no one trusts anyone else. The not-so-hidden agenda in this business is *"Get mine first."* This attitude ties everyone to a self-serving, conflicting agenda that is detrimental to each participant. Investors—the last in line—usually suffer the most, hence the abundance of horror stories about investors losing money in movie deals. The result: financing is the most difficult, convoluted stage in the film-making process.

Consequently the producer, in order to survive and to protect the investor, tries to get the largest possible advance. It's a hit-and-run, one-night stand philosophy that puts the small distributor in a terrible bind because a large advance cripples his resources for successful film marketing. Without a strong marketing push the picture's potential is limited.

These business practices have resulted in precedents that can hurt the very success of films everyone is gambling on. Each person in the chain does his or her best to pass on the risk to the next in line. It ends at the distributor, who has paid a big advance and must struggle for recoupment.

It's also important to get your distributor to commit to a release date. Since advances are often paid on release, if the film isn't released, there is no advance. Home video and television releases are often triggered months later by the theatrical release date. A film that isn't released is held up in all ancillary markets.

Some possible deal points between theatrical distributors and producers are:

1. The producer participates from gross receipts. This is hard to get because the distributor's costs may end up unrecouped.

2. The gross is split 70/30 or 60/40 between distributor and producer. The distributor deducts print and ad costs from his share.

3. The distributor deducts prints and ad costs and the split is 50/50. The problem here is that the distributor will be cautious in spending print and ad money, which can inhibit chances for the film's success.

There is no standard distribution deal. Everyone negotiates the best deal he can for himself. The better the picture, the more people who want it, and the better deal the producer should be able to make. The converse is also true.

FOREIGN FINANCING

Many producers go overseas to make their films. One reason is that there were once many tax incentives for investors. Few tax deals are left in the world, and those that remain have a complex list of regulations regarding financing, taxes, corporate structures, and registration, which means the producer has to hire an expert to guide him or her through the maze.

Still there is an advantage to producing abroad, which is that below-the-line crew costs can be paid in local currency. In countries where the dollar is still strong you can save from 10 to 30 percent of the below-the-line budget. This really makes sense only for high-budget movies in which the savings can be significant. Below-the-line equity deals that can also be made. (Conversely, where the dollar is weak provides great investment incentives for strong-currency investors such as the Japanese. No wonder they are investing in American films.) There are foreign sales reps and international packagers (usually law firms) that, for a fee, help make deals in foreign territories for co-productions and equity deals.

THE FINANCING ISSUE: Chicken or the Egg?

Producers are confused about where to start. They ask, *"Do I look for distribution first? Or do I look for financing?"* You probably look for both simultaneously. Here's one way to think about it.

Sometimes the only way you'll get financing is if you have a distributor step up for an advance against all rights (theatrical, home video, TV). That might be any of the independents or small studios. With distribution in place you may be able to induce investors to participate in a limited partnership. Their involvement will be predicated on the question, *"Who's distributing the picture?"* It's unrealistic to expect anyone to walk up with a million bucks until that question is answered. That means the equity investment is going to come after your distribution is in place—at the tail end. Unless you are independently wealthy or you have a lot of good friends, you aren't going get major financing until you've solved the issue of domestic distribution. You have to have a very good sense of who is interested in your picture domestically and close a distribution deal as quickly as you can so that you can start looking for investors.

A Pre-Sale Strategy

Foreign and domestic pre-sales are really essential because they will finance your picture. The only reason to turn to equity investment is if you can raise the whole amount up front, which will be hard unless you have a track record or you have to make up a shortfall from pre-sales. However, getting equity money from investors can be difficult if you've already sold all your rights worldwide. You've given away the

117

upside and there's no incentive for an investor to come aboard unless there are still unsold rights that will generate income for an investor's recoupment and profits. It's extremely complicated and intertwined and you have to find the best situation for your film.

One way to piece it all together is to selectively sell off territories. Pre-sell the U.S. to a single distributor and then pre-sell England, Japan, and France. If there is still a gap in your financing needs you've reserved Italy, Spain, West Germany, and a number of key territories. The investors will look to those territories as their primary source of recoupment.

Summary

Pre-sales unlock the doors for as much as 40 to 60percent of your budget, depending of course on the picture's genre and international appeal. Working together with foreign sales agents and building your package with appealing elements strengthen your film's potential. Producers might consider attending major films markets to understand how business is done internationally. More often than not, foreign pre-sales help leverage investment domestically if not too many markets have been sold off. A producer needs to evaluate his film's pre-sale potential and exactly how much upside should be sold off in order to finance his or her picture. A domestic distribution deal will increase the value of the film abroad. Most projects will need to be pieced together with financing from a variety of sources. Careful planning and thinking can help producers find the right course of action for their film.

BLOCKED
CURRENCY

BLOCKED CURRENCY

"The trick is to find it—and then liberate it."

Introduction

U.S. and other foreign corporations that do business in a foreign land are often prevented by local laws from exchanging their profit for other currencies and taking it out of the country, and so it must remain there in the form of the local currency. These monies are called *"blocked funds."* A strategy that allows the owner (individual or corporation) to get his money out of the country is using blocked funds to produce a film within the country, then exporting the film to earn the money to reimburse its costs and possibly generate profits. In short, this provides a way to convert profit held in the form of domestic money and get it out of the country. A lot of corporate money in the form of local currency is sitting around in foreign accounts. The trick is to find it—and liberate it.

This strategy is particularly appealing in countries where the dollar is strong and has a good exchange rate.

Another advantage is that a producer may be able to negotiate a price with the holders of blocked currency that is better than the official exchange rate. After all, the holders may be delighted to get it off their hands. For example, a producer might purchase a portion of foreign blocked funds at a discount greater than the foreign exchange rate. This increases the producer's ability to get even greater value for his money. A U.S. corporation may be happy to do this in order to get U.S. dollars.

121

While conceptually this seems easy, some producers say that getting to blocked funds can be a life's work. The cost of lawyers for these deals is expensive.

Foreign co-productions with blocked currency exist today in Yugoslavia, Algeria, Ireland, and the Soviet Union.

DEBT EQUITY: STEPHEN CUNNINGHAM INTERVIEW

Stephen Cunningham is a managing director at Bear Stearns, an investment banking firm in Manhattan. He is experienced in the world of blocked funds and debt swapping and in the following interview provides a clear and detailed understanding of how this complex financing works.

What is debt equity?

"As the term is used today, debt equity means the conversion of commercial bank indebtedness into an equity stake in a country by exchanging local currency for the dollar equivalent (or some discount from the dollar equivalent of par) of the outstanding dollar indebtedness. A Mexican asset that trades in the international debt markets at a price of (to use an example) 40 cents on the dollar is exchanged for shares by converting or contributing that debt instrument in a local Mexican company, whereby the government finances or provides local currency at a maximum local-currency equivalent of about (in this example) 65 cents on the dollar.

"Brazil created the original debt equity program. It restructured its debt and offered creditors an exchange of existing debt for the equivalent in local currency in one of two ways: first, either through a debt equity conversion whereby a multinational company buys that debt instrument from the bank at (for example) a price of 80, contributes it to its local subsidiary, and is credited by the central bank with a price of 100; or second, the multinational buys the debt

122

instrument from the bank at 80, contributes it as an intercompany parent to subsidiary loan, and picks up the differential of between 80 and 100.

"The term *debt to equity* is a broad term used differently in different countries. Its basic concept is that international debts of many countries trade in a very active secondary market. Many countries created these 'debt equity programs' and used them to 1) extinguish off-shore debt by enabling people to acquire and convert it, or 2) contribute it to an equity position in that country. Governments agreed to underwrite this by ostensibly paying off that debt in local currency—sometimes par and sometimes through a process that auctioned off grants of company debt equity conversions to the highest bidder. The governments said, 'We'll offer X number of debt equity rights this particular quarter to the people who give us the greatest discount from par.' From the government standpoint, they began to work it down from par. Instead of saying only 'I'll do it for 100,' executives were so anxious to pump capital into their company that they offered 99, or 98, or 97, etc."

Who is holding the debt in these countries?

"Right now, most of the debt is held by the international commercial banks. It is owed by the government's central bank or by different governmental agencies."

So they're saying, "Rather than repay this in dollars, which is going to break our backs, we'll give you some of the local currency at a discount but you have to use it in our local economy." It's a great break for somebody who wants to do business in Brazil.

"Right, and normally there are restrictions depending on how you take advantage of the debt conversion program. What do I mean by that? If you convert it into equity, debt conversion usually follows foreign investment regulations tied to restrictions on repatriation of capital, and in some cases to the limit on the amount of dividends that can be remitted from a dollar-registered capital base in that country. If you convert this into a parent/subsidiary loan, it usually follows the payment schedule adopted by the banks."

Is your company, Bear Stearns, the agent?

"Bear Stearns has played a lot of roles in debt swap and started in this during 1984. We had two roles.

"First, we served as advisors to a lot of these companies, informing them of the debt equity programs and working with them on structuring conversions. That meant bringing the firms up the learning curve on how to avail themselves of the debt equity program, and helping them go through the central bank to get the debt instruments approved. We let multinationals know of these programs and worked with a number of companies who were headquartered in the U.S., Europe, and Asia.

"Second, we provided an agency role of going out and sourcing the debt at the cheapest levels. This is a form of 'debt swap.' Clearly one can just go out and buy the debt, but another way is to swap the debt between different banks, which sometimes provides you with the substantial additional advantage of acquiring the debt at a price cheaper than paying cash."

Give an example of two partners that might get together to swap.

"For accounting reasons different banks may globally value assets unequally within different countries, and you get them to do an exchange. One bank may value an asset at one price and another bank at a slightly different price, so you offer the end acquirer of that asset a better price. In some cases you can offer the seller of that asset a higher price than if you were going to sell it straight for cash because he's not receiving cash directly, but another asset that he may value higher than the cash equivalent."

Give an example of how a motion picture company could take advantage of debt equity and/or a debt swap conversion.

"The film company sets up a subsidiary in a country in which it intends to produce the movie or any aspect of the entire film process. Let's assume that it costs $10 million to produce the film in any given country but let's use Mexico as an example. The easiest way would be to have the film company pay U.S. dollars (or else borrow from a U.S. bank), and with it acquire a Mexican asset that qualified for the debt equity conversion program. It acquires an asset (Mexican restructured bank loan). Let's take Mexico at today's market prices of 42 cents.

"Assume that the government is willing to allow that asset to be converted at a price of 65. So, following through on the example, if the film company needs approximately $10 million of local currency, it would effectively need only $6 or $7 million.

"The film company takes that asset (the Mexican bank loan) and retires it with the government. It says, 'I am giving you this asset, for which you will provide to me the equivalent (say the negotiated 65 cents level) in local currency.' The government makes that currency available to the film company, which then uses it for labor, construction, production, whatever, and has the right to '*repatriate*' any earnings from the operation that it produced in Mexico over a specified period of time, according to the debt conversion process in place in Mexico.

"Repatriate" means that when the debt is converted into capital (most of the countries have foreign investment guidelines that govern the ability to withdraw capital that has been brought into a country) there is an agreement on how money may be taken back out of the country.

"See, all the film company has done is reduce the cost of producing this film by effectively taking advantage of the discount."

Buying cheaper dollars. Buying pesos.

"Right. Now, how the firm repays the dollars it used is a function of the sales price of the film, how many movie theaters the film plays at, and the marketing rights of the film.

"The U.S. film company makes this debt equity conversion into the local subsidiary, thereby having, according to the Mexican government, an equity contribution in its local subsidiary. They can leave that there and ignore it. It may not have any real benefit to the company. It's all a question of how the company goes about paying for the production of the film. I started off my example with a film company that had $6 or $7 million but needed $10 million to produce the film in Mexico. So it would take cash out of the parent, buy the debt in the secondary market, convert it into equity in a local subsidiary that it created in the country, and then effectively receive $10 million equivalent in local currency.

"Let's assume they didn't have the whole $6 or $7 million. What they do in that case is to go out and borrow the equivalent amount of dollars, again buy the debt, and again contribute it. They must repay the dollars they borrowed either through revenue from the film or through any other revenue generated from the whole production process of the film."

Say you don't have the money and you don't want to borrow the money. You only want to put up some cash. Can you get the governments to take equity in the production itself?

"No, that's kind of tough. I have not really seen an example of a government participating as an equity partner. What you can do is get people to lend you the debt (instead of cash) that is used for the conversion. What do I mean by that? Let's assume that you're a U.S. bank and hold this debt that, according to the secondary market value, is worth 42 cents. Now, what if you lent that debt to Michael Wiese Productions, which capitalizes that debt into a Mexican subsidiary of Michael Wiese Productions and produces a film? Depending on the revenue coming from the film that Michael Wiese produced down there, you might be able to generate enough revenue in the future to repay the debt that the U.S. commercial bank lent you.

"You can see why it's a benefit to the bank. The bank goes from a sovereign risk asset sitting there with a value of, let's say, 42, to a higher asset, a loan to Michael Wiese Productions, that may produce a film and sell it in dollars. Thus, the bank will be able to see a dollar revenue stream that can eventually be used to repay the sovereign risk asset it gave to Michael Wiese Productions."

This vehicle must be used all the time. It's very attractive.

"It was most heavily used by most major film companies, principally in Mexico, and got its most active use in the tourism sector. The reason is that all sorts of Americans and Europeans, as well as Asians, love to visit the coast of Mexico. So tourism operators and developers would construct hotels and get the banks to contribute the debt along the lines I've just described to you. And the banks would look at a payout from the American Express card receipts or dollar revenues that these hotels would generate over time from the flood of tourism."

And that's how all these developing countries got locked into tourism as much as they have?

"That's right. Tourism is a dollar-generating type of investment. Let's say you were talking about a company that wanted to produce lollipops for the local population. Well, here your risks are

127

substantial. The company to which you contribute the debt on the lollipops is selling those lollipops in Mexico in pesos. There are no dollar revenues to offset the dollar indebtedness that is contributed. You've got to hope the company not only has a strong lollipop sales base but can also convert the pesos into dollars to repay the loans it lent you."

What about blocked funds? How do they figure into this?

"Blocked funds work in a variety of ways but are most useful in countries with currency controls. For example, blocked funds are not useful in Mexico because you have a free peso exchange rate. In Mexico, anybody with pesos can buy dollars at any bank."

So blocked-fund financing techniques work best in countries in which there are restrictions on converting local currencies into dollars and taking them out of the country?

"To make a blocked-funds deal work, you need companies with a substantial amount of local currency in a country that restricts local-currency conversion into hard currency. Brazil is an example. A multi-national company selling a lot of products there can generate a substantial amount of local currency but cannot convert it into dollars to send to its parent company. Why? Brazil stringently restricts the amount of its currency that can be converted into dollars. These restrictions are related to the dollar capital position the multinational company has in its local subsidiary."

Doesn't this relate to the strength of the local currency that we're talking about here and the possibility that if a company starts taking it out in any given quantity.

"You're right. You get into a situation where the foreign currency reserves of the country are affected. If a country's foreign currency reserves are in a difficult position, the central bank of that country may not have enough hard currency to meet the needs of companies who might simultaneously want to convert into hard currency the substantial amount of excess local currency they have generated."

Is it mostly corporate money that is blocked?

"Yes. Stating it simplistically, the transaction could look like this for a producer: When you're talking about blocked funds, you're normally referring to countries with relatively restrictive currency controls that create what is called a parallel market. So you have an official market and a parallel market for currency."

Or a black market?

"Yes. Obviously dollars cost a substantial premium at the official exchange rate because they are difficult to acquire. In the parallel market you're able to pick up local currency at a substantial discount. Say a U.S. film company wants to produce a film in Brazil and discovers its costs will be $10 million in local currency. The film company would say, 'I need the equivalent of $10 million in local currency.' A multinational would say, 'I have $10 million in local currency in my subsidiary that I will give you for a dollar value that equals what the parallel market will pay my parent here in the U.S.'"

And everybody wins. Except perhaps the local government?

"Right. But most multinationals do not participate in that kind of a transaction. Why? Because in essence they would be breaking the currency laws of the countries they are operating in. So what happens? They make use of a number of legal mechanisms that may take advantage of the parallel market but fall within the laws of the particular country."

These are very sophisticated transactions.

"Yes. The financial engineering used is not as straightforward as simply having Michael Wiese Productions write a check for $7 million to XYZ multinational in the U.S., whereupon XYZ tells its local subsidiary to provide $10 million of local currency to Michael Wiese Productions in that country. A number of steps in between must be taken to comply with currency restrictions. But the end result is the same."

Is a $10-million film a large enough deal for a company like yours to get involved? On what scale does this start to make sense?

"$10 million is definitely something we would have an interest in, but I've got to be up front with you, Michael. Dealing with blocked currencies is not something that Bear Stearns really focuses on. We are active in debt equities and debt swaps but refrain from participating in blocked currency transactions. People strong in that area tend to be some of the major international law firms and some of the larger commercial banks. I can recommend a law firm called Baker, McKenzie in New York."

What countries offer the best opportunities for debt equity or debt swap?

"It's a moving target. If you ask me who's got a debt equity program today, Venezuela and Chile are two countries that immediately come to mind. Mexico had a debt equity program after its new restructuring, and I'm sure that with the election of its new government, Brazil will reinstate its program. But a place like Argentina, which had one, does not have one today. Nor does Brazil right now. Most of the Eastern European countries, such as Yugoslavia, Czechoslovakia, and Hungary, are in the process of creating debt equity programs. In the Far East, the major program is the Philippines, not Thailand."

Who are the debt equity program players in the world besides your company?

"The Bank of Boston, Security Pacific Bank, and a large Dutch bank that goes by the acronym NMB. Some of the big commercial banks like Citibank, Chase, and Morgan are also players. The people you want to meet are in the Latin American corporate finance departments of these banks."

Does your company work on a percentage of the raise, say 6 percent, and a retainer?

"Yes, it's done on a retainer basis with a percentage of the amount raised. The fees on raising this kind of financing are not what scares off the producer; the problem is paying any kind of a retainer, even a minimal amount."

Because they're not in business yet.

"Exactly right. They're not turned off by the percentage on the amount of debt raised, which is a lot less than the amount you quoted me."

Does that include all the business affairs and all the legal...

"No. Legal and everything else is separate. Those are just the straight costs, call them the banking fees."

Do these deals usually stick, or do a high ratio of them fall apart? Is it really a way for producers to go?

"It is, but again, it's such a moving target, at least in my experience. The dialogue with a number of film companies that come to us goes something like this: 'I'd like to produce a picture in X country. Is there a debt equity program? Fine, there's a debt equity program. OK, how does it work?' To determine how the debt equity program will work for this particular film producer, we ask, 'Do you have a film?' The producer says, 'Well, I've got three or four films.' 'And which one are you going to produce there?' we ask. 'I don't know yet,' he says. 'Can you help me with the financing to acquire the debt to do the debt equity conversion?' All this takes time, and the small independent producers seem to get disillusioned and go other routes."

Let's say that the producer wants to shoot an action picture but your company is just not able to get a deal in any of those countries you mentioned. It's taken a while to discover this. Is the producer racking up tens of thousands of dollars in fees to find out?

"On the retainer side? Yes, he is."

But if you make it work, it's worth it.

"Yes, that's the whole point. The cost savings are astronomical."

From your side, is it expensive to stay current with these ever-changing international situations?

"We need to stay current on debt equity. Again, blocked funds is something we do not participate in—we've built a reputation in debt equity programs. And not only with the small, independent film companies—we were doing debt equity deals for most of the Fortune 500 long before anybody else was aware of them. Now the process is so well known it's gotten to the point where we handle the major companies at the international treasurer level."

Besides yourself, how many others handle debt equity programs?

"Today the top 15 U.S. banks have debt equity program specialists in most of the countries that use debt equity. Several Wall Street houses like ourselves have people who understand these programs. A whole series of boutique specialists have sprung up. A large number of

European banks are involved, as are many European brokerage firms. It's an active business with a number of people."

Thank you, Stephen Cunningham.

TOM RAUTENBERG INTERVIEW

Tom Rautenberg provides financial consulting to motion picture and television producers. Sometimes he functions as an investment banker or producer's rep. In the following interview, he shares some of his experience in working with blocked funds.

Give me an example of a blocked-fund situation and what corporations do to liberate their cash from these countries.

"Take the Soviet Union. When a company like Pepsi Cola or McDonald's goes into that country and is earning rubles all day long, all of them can't be spend constructively inside the country, so it has to find ways to convert the rest into a commodity. The firm looks for something it can purchase, invest in, or manufacture–like a motion picture, which can be exported to the outside world and earn hard currency. You need to deal directly, either with companies you've identified that are operating in the country, or, if you know you will be in the Soviet Union or Yugoslavia or Brazil, with local groups like national film commissions, which can help you identify American corporations that might looking for a motion picture vehicle."

Have you done any of these?

"I've done one, but unfortunately I'm not allowed to talk about it. It's with a major company that doesn't want any publicity."

How does the local corporation, the Pepsi or McDonald's, evaluate the movie?

Who looks out for its interests?

"Usually, either there's an individual in the treasurer's department of the company whose major job is 'liberating' funds overseas, or the firm has a relationship with a major investment banking group such as Bear Sterns that does it for them.

"I'll give you a real-world example. An Italian publisher, Rizzoli, is entering into a joint venture agreement with the Soviet government to publish a women's magazine. The firm is going to earn rubles and will be able to buy a lot of paper with them, but plans on having to retain a lot of rubles So Rizzoli asked, `How do we find a credible company with products we can invest in that will give us a good chance of getting our money back?' The answer revolved around finding a producer with a track record or a well-established co-production partner. The publisher is now in discussion with a number of 'established' television and film companies that want to create joint ventures with the Soviet Union. That's what the corporation or the bank is going to be looking for."

I would think that just about any movie deal would terrify bankers and corporations.

"You'd be surprised. A lot of people consider movies a very good way to get currency out of a country. The reasons are twofold. First, movies do very well in general. People don't understand that movies are not as bad an investment as they might think. Second, movies have long-term asset play."

Such as library value?

"Yes, and as these libraries build, even on inexpensive films, and as markets mature, which has happened in the last five or ten years in Southeast Asia, this asset gains value. Suddenly countries like Malaysia, Korea, and Thailand are buying product that will recoup a substantial amount of the original investment over time. Obviously an opportunity cost is involved here, but you have to understand that many corporations in foreign countries are sitting on soft currency they're never going to use. Sometimes it's been there for years."

What are the countries where these deals are made?

"They're mostly third world or eastern bloc countries. One place where there's some currency is India. India is interesting because the country produces more motion pictures than virtually anywhere else in the world. So if you come up with an interesting idea for doing something in India, there are companies available."

Was RAZOR'S EDGE done in India with block funds?

"I think so. Certainly the producers of GANDHI were putting some deals together. I think the British commonwealth banks were handling that. The long-term appreciation of these assets is pretty good in terms of not losing money or principal over the long run. We're not talking about the cheapie stuff; we're talking about something that has a little asset value—$2 million or above."

But don't most people that invest in movies want a quick return?

"Surprisingly, there are corporations who've been sitting on foreign currency or bad debt for years. Their attitude is a little different from that of a traditional investor. If you can find the right group that has debt, it will sometimes sell you local currency at 30 cents on the dollar. And perhaps negotiate a deal to provide you with $2 million worth of Brazilian currency. Oftentimes you can do the deal where, look, it's a $4-million picture, we'll cover your entire below the line, but we want to be a 50 percent partner. So all of a sudden they're getting a picture and getting credited with full value for something they could get only 30 cents on the dollar for in the open market."

And the producer would make that deal in a minute. A producer can have still further benefit on the foreign exchange?

"Potentially."

What other products besides motion pictures are block funds being used for?

"A lot of times they swap it for natural resources: oil, tin, lumber— something they can get cash for elsewhere in the world."

Then why are so many blocked funds still sitting around?

"One reason is that raw goods must often be purchased in such large quantities that swapping becomes prohibitive."

So a producer might go to a foreign trade commission, identify corporations in that country, go down the list to company number one hundred and one, and start there.

"Exactly. You do your homework and find out who's in the country where you want to shoot. The hard part is that banks are not that interested in a small independent walking in the door."

How can a producer with a smaller, independent film get blocked– or debt-fund financing if it's a one-time only proposition and he doesn't know the bankers?

"Unless you've got friends, or unless banks think you're going to be doing more business with foreign banks or corporations, it's very hard. One of the advantages a producer's rep or a small investment banker has is that he frequently works with and has an ongoing relationship with bigger banks. As a producer's rep myself, I can work with a number of banks on debt or block currency because I represent four or five different production groups, all of who might need that service at one point or another."

What do you do for your clients?

"Sometimes I help structure the deal. Sometimes I consult, recommending a strategy that the client carries out. Sometimes I do it on the client's behalf, which makes me a producer's rep. Sometimes I'm doing 'investment banking' by putting the financing together. The hats change depending on how much I'm involved in structuring the capital. At the most involved level, I do investment banking; at the middle level, when I'm connecting capital sources, I'm a producer's rep; and at the third level, when I'm helping create plans for people to get money, I act as a financial consultant."

Thank you, Tom Rautenberg.

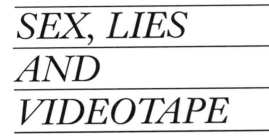

SEX, LIES
AND
VIDEOTAPE

"SEX, LIES, AND VIDEOTAPE"
A Financial Case Study

"I didn't think it was a commercial movie at all."

Robert Newmyer Interview

Robert Newmyer was an executive producer on the independent feature SEX, LIES AND VIDEOTAPE. This film is a model for many independent producers because it: 1) was a very good film, 2) was an "art film" that crossed over, 3) was produced independently, 4) was written and directed by a first timer, and 5) generated enormous profits from a low-production budget. The film exemplifies the American independent producer's dream.

The producer's approach to financing and production serves as a model to many independents, although even SEX, LIES... producer Robert Newmyer warns that the film was a rarity—everything *"just worked."*

An unusual deal structure allowed the budget to be raised from a home video company and through foreign pre-sales. The basic rule of "you need to have a theatrical distributor" was broken as there was no certainty how the film would be distributed theatrically when it was being financed.

Newmyer is a producer whose ace is his ability to locate new writers and directors and help them develop and structure their material. He is also an astute deal maker, and worked many years analyzing deal structures as vice president of production and acquisitions for Columbia. The strengths of his partners, Stan Brooks and Jeff Silver, are in the physical production of films and development.

141

This combination enables the triad to operate a company with a relatively small overhead and devote the time necessary to ferret out good quality motion picture stories, screenplays, and talent.

My interview with Newmyer reveals what happens when you have a combination of savvy producer skills, a strong production team, favorable festival reviews, and lots of good luck.

How did you find SEX, LIES, AND VIDEOTAPE?

"The very first script that the company optioned was something called DEATH FROM THE NECK UP, which was written by Steve Soderbergh. We didn't know who he was but the script made us laugh a lot, so we optioned it. We flew Steve out here and started developing it with him with no idea that he was an aspiring director.

"Steve made four or five trips, coming out once every three weeks over a three-month period, and we worked with him developing and redeveloping the script. We really liked working with Steve and once that script was in shape (before we even started to try to get financing), we suggested that he write another script for us, sort of an American version of a James Bond film. Rather than continually flying him out here, we said, *'Look, why don't we just give you enough money to get in a car and drive out and stay out here?'*

"Steve got in his car, a $400 beat-up white Buick, and started driving from Baton Rouge. He thought of SEX, LIES... while he was driving, and wrote the first draft on the road, in cheap motel rooms and picnic benches. By the time he arrived five days later, he threw the completed script on our desk. So all of a sudden we had three projects, one of which, SEX, LIES..., had never been normally optioned."

So you started with the script. What did you do next?

"First we budgeted the script and got a rough idea of the cost. I had worked at Columbia so I knew the people at RCA/Columbia home video, and that was the first place we went. They immediately said they would do it because we said we could make it for a million dollars. They liked Steve, they liked us, we had a 'go' movie.

"They gave us half the budget—$600,000—in cash for the home video rights. Today RCA/Columbia does it in the form of paper and producers have to go to the banks. But we got cash. We also got a contractual guarantee that RCA/Columbia would put up $500,000 of the print and advertising money if necessary.

"As it turned out, RCA/Columbia actually funded the entire $1.2 million movie. They were only at risk for $600,000 because they knew that we had a foreign pre-sale in place with Virgin for the other half of the money, which we assigned to RCA/Columbia.

"At that point the history is a lot more complicated, because Steve changed his mind. He decided he wanted to make the film in black and white, not in color, and we had a major falling out. He went off and tried to make it in black and white with other producers (all of whom eventually became executive producers on this picture).

"Steve came back about four months later and said *'Okay, I wasn't able to do it. How about if we go back to RCA/Columbia?'* And I said, *'Fine, but we're going to produce the movie.'*

"It was a simple production. Steve was very fiscally responsible. The film was made at a low budget because Steve had so many favors to call upon, and because he had a terrific line producer."

143

What's your deal with RCA, the other financiers and the actors?

"RCA acted just as a studio would act. All the money that was earned by that picture from every source goes through RCA/Columbia until they recoup their investment. In other words, all the Virgin foreign pre-sale money goes to RCA, including any overages, plus all the Miramax theatrical money, including the advances plus the overages, plus all the RCA video money. The net of the fee that Miramax and Virgin take goes through Columbia. Once RCA recoups its $1.2 million we split the rest. And there will be a lot of overages. We gave a lot of points to the actors and the crew in return for reduced salaries. The executive producers share in profits. Although the pie is split a lot of ways, ultimately at least $4 or $5 million in profit participations will be paid out on this picture.

"We had a completion bond. RCA left us alone and we left Steve alone. I went down to the set but was not particularly active. Steve had things well in hand, and this was such a personal movie, so much his personal vision—unlike the next movie we're going to make that will make people laugh, and where I think I'll be very active on the set. But on this one there was nothing I could do but leave him alone and try not to get in his way."

When the film was finished, you didn't have a distributor. How did you find one?

"The next step was the premiere. Steve took a very wet print—I mean dripping wet—on an airplane to the Park City Film Festival where we premiered it. We got an enormous response, an enormous amount of interest from various distributors. In fact, many of the majors were interested in distributing it, pending our buying back the video rights from RCA, which was not possible. And we met with virtually every other distributor except the majors.

144

"Theatrical, pay and syndication were the only rights left. We met with each distributor and asked how they'd release it, what they thought it would do, worst-case and best-case scenarios. Goldwyn and Island were probably the most serious distributors.

"At the end of meeting with everybody, we had been pitched all sorts of deals. One had a higher advance, one had a higher per net commitment, one had a higher share of the gross, one had a higher share of the net. The deals were like apples and oranges—there was no way to compare them. So we sat down and decided what we needed in terms of print and ad commitment, of approvals over the marketing campaign and distribution pattern, of profit participation.

"RCA had approval over the deal but there was no disagreement—it was a great working relationship. I used to do these financial models for Columbia—I was the one that modeled the deals and then we reviewed them. It's not as if we had divergent interests. So we set the terms. We took the highest advance."

This is incredibly rare. How did you go about getting a theatrical distributor when you had already sold the video rights?

"For these deals to happen with video rights already attached is really unheard of these days. (See 'Split Rights' at end of this chapter.) We were just lucky that we got Steve, that Steve got involved, and that we made a great picture. I would not want to take this bet again. When you get a picture with only theatrical, pay, and syndication rights left, you're not going to get a bidding war going. We got extremely lucky. Miramax took all the remaining rights in SEX, LIES... pay, syndication, and theatrical. They advanced roughly $1 million.

"We got ourselves into a situation that could have been problematic because we had stripped video rights. The more likely deal we would have had to accept was one in which RCA/Columbia advanced the

145

cost of releasing theatrically. In our case, RCA was able to control the theatrical rights without paying for them by locking up home video and by effectively financing the total cost of the picture. Even though Virgin came up with the other half of the budget, RCA had laid it all out. At one point, before they got back half of the money from Virgin, RCA had invested $1.1 million on this picture."

[Note: To recap, the financial sources for the $1.2 million film were 1) RCA/Columbia: $600,000 for domestic home video rights (plus $500,000 print and advertising, if necessary); 2) Virgin: $600,000 for all rights foreign; 3) Miramax: $1,000,000 advance for pay, syndication, and theatrical rights following the premiere. The Virgin and Miramax money flowed back through RCA until recoupment.—M.W.]

What were the elements that made you think this was a commercial movie?

"I didn't think it was a commercial movie at all, I didn't have a clue about that. I thought that it would be an interesting foreign art house film that would open in Los Angeles and in New York and have an extremely long run because the subject matter was so provocative. I thought it would do extremely well, maybe $2, $3, or $4 million in 10 or 20 theaters in major markets only. I never imagined in my wildest dreams that it would go wider than 5 cities and 20 theaters."

And the final result?

"Ultimately, it was in 535 theaters and grossed a little over $24 million. Most of that was generated by word of mouth. There was no television advertising. A studio would have spent $8 million on the release, but Miramax spent next to nothing to release it, just for striking the prints and flying people around for publicity."

What do you expect it to do in video sales?

"I'd be disappointed if it didn't do 120,000, but it could do 150,000. But that's not my area of expertise. "

Tell me about your next project and how you plan to finance it?

"A very low-budget film—RULES OF THE GAME—was brought to us by a friend of mine named Stan Brooks. We partnered with him and optioned the script from the screenwriter and the agency for practically no money. We knew we could do this for a couple million dollars, exclusive of producing fees, so we decided we would defer all of our fees—take no money whatsoever out of it—and raise funds privately. We raised $2 million from 32 private investors. We're in pre-production and casting.

"We had a script. We did not have any cast, any director. We raised the $2 million after SEX, LIES...had been licensed to Miramax but before it won the Palm d'Or at the Cannes Film Festival. It was already a substantially profitable picture.

"We have a very short track record, but at least we had one. We were also partners with Stan Brooks, who brought us the project. He is a very successful television producer who produced five television movies for about the same budget of $2 to $3 million. My other permanent partner, Jeff Silver, is a line producer who used to run physical production for Cannon Pictures and has line-produced a lot of pictures, including 52 PICKUP, TOUGH GUYS DON'T DANCE, and SHAG. The combination of Stan and Jeff gave investors confidence that if we said we could make a movie for $2 million, we really could. I think SEX, LIES... also gave investors confidence that we had some taste for what might be commercial.

"We also knew a lot of people, mostly through my connections, although I probably knew only 10 of the 32 investors personally. When we went about raising the money, we asked five people I knew who had some interest, all of whom were lawyers or doctors or in the

147

real estate business. And each of those five knew another five, and those five knew another five. They put up a low of $25,000 to a high of $200,000, with the average being about $75,000.

"We set three meetings in Washington at one of the initial investors' offices. We called everyone and said we were calling at the suggestion of so-and-so, this is what it's about, if you have any interest please come. We'd give them a verbal pitch over the phone. Then we came with a business plan and gave an hour-long presentation, describing who we were, what the picture was about, and how we intended to market and distribute the picture.

How does the deal with your investors work?

"The deal is very simple. Investors get back 125 percent of their investment. So if someone puts in $100,000 he gets back $125,000 before anybody takes a dime. Then we take our producer's fees, which are modest. Then we pay those who deferred portions of their compensation, which includes the director, the writer, and most of the actors. After that, we split 50/50 with the investors. We'll end up giving away about half of our 50 percent, or 25 percent of the total, to a combination of everybody else. As producers we'll probably end up with 25 percent of the profits.

"This is an unusual deal because **we don't intend to negotiate a distribution deal until after we finish the picture.** We have no downside protection. It's risky for two reasons. One, we have not pre-sold any rights so there's no guarantee of a dime coming back if it's a terrible picture. And two, unlike many low-budget pictures ours is not an action film, and does not have the elements that give it international appeal. It's a straight American-based comedy geared toward American audiences. If you make a low-budget action picture, you may get a million dollars or more for the foreign rights. **If our film is bad and doesn't work, the foreign rights will be worthless.**

"We will get some foreign sales, but the real upside is that if it's a good picture we'll get it distributed through a mini-major or, though unlikely, through a major studio.

"The idea is to get a domestic distributor since we'll have all the domestic rights available, including video. We hope to get a U.S.-based distributor to guarantee a decent expenditure on prints and ads.

"I'd love a major to pick it up but that's unlikely on a $2 million picture. The likely distributors that we would go to first are Miramax, New Line, and the Goldwyn Company. Those are probably the top three independent distributors who actually have a real chance of getting a picture out in more than 500 theaters.

"We were incredibly lucky to splinter rights on SEX, LIES AND VIDEOTAPE. The odds of getting real aggressive theatrical distribution for a low-budget picture when you've already stripped away video are one in a hundred. I fully expected SEX, LIES... to go out in ten theaters nationwide. I thought no one was going to give it an aggressive theatrical push if there were no video rights. Why should they build up the value of it for video without being able to reap the benefits?"

How will you open your new picture?

"We're torn about this. We may open it at the U.S. Film Festival. It's intended to be a very commercial picture that appeals to art film lovers. All the jury prizes and audience prizes at the U.S. Film Festival go to art pictures. The film will be at the Sundance film festival in Park City, Utah next year.

"While I think our comedy will play well to audiences, I'm not sure it will play particularly well to art audiences nor do I think it will win

149

any awards at that festival. So given that, I'm not sure we will open there. Instead, we might rent the Academy theater and invite our friends and everybody associated with the picture, as well as all the various potential buyers. We may spend $5,000 on this and a big party.

"I've never seen an independent picture premiered that way without a distributor. There are pretty compelling reasons to do it, one, because it's not really a festival picture, and two, because it is comedic. The appeal of the film is not particularly in the plot or the characters but in the laughs above and beyond the story and characters. You really care about the laughs, and if you screen this film to only five people at a time with potential distributors watching, you're asking for trouble.

"There's something about having an audience for a comedy that's infectious, which even was the case for SEX, LIES... People saw it with an audience and there was actual laughter. When you see SEX, LIES... in a room with five people, it plays very dramatic and downbeat. And this will certainly be even more so with this new movie.

"When I was at Columbia I saw all the pictures submitted for acquisition. I watched them in a room alone and none of the comedies played well for me. It's tough to get someone to laugh alone. So I think we'll probably rent a large room, host a huge screening, and seek distribution by inviting everybody."

What about a foreign sales deal to bring in some financing?

"We will probably make the domestic deal first because I think international buyers don't have a lot of judgment about how a picture is going to do, particularly a comedy. They tend to rely on how it does in the U.S.

"The foreign deal is really advance driven. We might rent a suite at one of the film festivals and sell it territory by territory ourselves. We'll consult with someone who's done it before. The alternative is to make a deal with one foreign sales distributor and get as large an advance as possible against profits, since it's difficult to audit foreign box office receipts and the advance might be all we'll ever see. The foreign sales rep will sell home video, television, and theatrical."

And foreign television syndication rights?

"It's possible now to hold foreign syndication rights and sell off video and theatrical. We'll talk to some really smart people about this. Not only have I not done this before but the market changes so quickly that there might be a whole different set of new deal structures available in Europe. I really don't think that is true for the domestic market, which is fairly static and I can anticipate the types of deals that will be available."

If you were to give strategic advice to a new feature producer what would you emphasize?

"I'm not in a great position to give advice to producers starting out, because if we hadn't been lucky with SEX, LIES... we would probably be out of business. The odds are against any one producer unless he is a studio producer. That's the only way to do it where the odds aren't against you. What that means is that you become an agent for a long time, make all your contacts, and then become a producer. The studio gives you a staff and an office in return for first right to see anything you want to develop.

"Or you can become a studio executive for years and years until you become senior vice president of production, and then they give you a deal. The studio funds your overhead. Because they're funding your overhead they're predisposed to want to do business with you. If they don't do business with you, they're just laying out the overhead for nothing and there's no downside to you. You're getting paid a salary, you have no costs, and things you want to develop you take to the studio to be funded. And if you can't find a studio that's willing to develop a piece of property, you don't go after it. It's the no-risk way of producing.

"What we did was put our own money on the line. I think you have to be lucky."

What about Steve Soderbergh's next picture?

"We had to go to the studio on Steve Soderbergh's next picture because it's so expensive. It's with Universal and likely to be at least a $10 million picture. And the other movie that we're in preproduction with is an $8 million picture with HBO. So we're not exclusively low-budget producers—we are exclusively non-union producers. The HBO film is an all-rights deal. They'll theatrically distribute through Warner Bros."

How do you go about developing properties? How do you compete with the well-financed studios?

"As a development/production company there are two things we had going for us. One was, we had relationships with all the agencies—the second tier agencies beyond William Morris and ICM. There's another tier of 15 or 20 agencies that we call every week. We solicit more material than you could imagine, spend all our time reading. We do find some diamonds in the rough. If you start out you're not going to get material as a first-time producer or even a second-time producer—we still don't get it through Creative Artists unless it's been seen by everyone else around town. So you have to do a lot of work to find the diamonds.

"You can be the first to get the second-tier agencies material if you're aggressive enough and they feel you can do something with it, particularly if they think you can improve the material. We don't just option screenplays and shop them, we develop them. We're usually dealing with raw talent or very funny dialogue writers who don't have much sense of story or structure. We make suggestions and improvements to a story, but we can't write the words.

"So we went into each of these agencies and pitched ourselves very hard. We told them that we were looking for young first-time comedic writers willing to develop material with us and that we weren't going to pay a fortune for it. We got mounds and mounds of material. It was a lot of work to find Steve Soderbergh, who came after reading a thousand scripts. Nobody knew who he was, but his script was fantastic.

"We are willing to spend our own money on options. We did not want to go around and pitch the studios for a development deal. We probably spent a total of only $100,000 in two years. Our average is $5,000 or $10,000 a deal, so it wasn't a lot of money. But it did mean that we went for a year and a half without earning any money and spending $100,000.

"And we were doing this more than full time. All I was doing was reading screenplays and working with those writers we found, all of whom were and are very much like Steve in writing capacity. And then we controlled the material and we thought it was good, so we were really very much a screenplay-based company.

"There are a lot of people using this strategy. I think we're probably one of the most aggressive and we are also a full-service operation. We have the capability not just to option a screenplay and develop it, but can also physically make it. We also have picture-making skills. I know how to make the deals and my partner can physically produce the films. Between us we have all of the divergent skills that make us a real producing house. **Most producers on their own are either strong in physical production or development or deal making.** I think it is unusual to find a company strong in all three of them. The basis of our trying to get material is pitching that to the agencies all the time. "

As a independent producer, what's an argument that you can make for working outside the studios?

"If you are making pictures that are financed by studios, you are basically in it for producer fees and give up any chance of profit participation. That's not going to get you to the point where you really can raise money privately unless you have a long and successful track record at a studio, like Larry Gordon like Joel Silver or Guber-Peters. That's years and years, and you need ten successful pictures.

"If your goal is to raise a pool of private investment money, which is what we'd like to do, and you do it on one small picture and make money, if you do what we're doing and raise $2 million and give investors back $4 million, then suddenly do it again on a $4 million picture, then maybe you can raise $20 million. If you don't screw it up, the time frame is shorter.

"If the next movie we do privately works, in two years we can raise $20 or $30 million privately. But if we foul up the picture we're doing independently, we're out of being able to raise money privately for a decade. So we're a little nervous about it."

Thank you, Robert Newmyer.

FINANCING
HIGH QUALITY
INDEPENDENT FILMS

FINANCING HIGH QUALITY INDEPENDENT FILMS

"In the FilmDallas scheme, the first thing we did is take the decision about the individual investments out of the investor's hands."

Sam Grogg Interview

Sam Grogg founded FilmDallas, a financing, producing and distribution company which invested in a series of motion pictures including KISS OF THE SPIDER WOMAN which was nominated for four Academy Awards, and TRIP TO BOUNTIFUL, which was nominated for two Academy Awards. His producing credits include THE TRIP TO BOUNTIFUL, PATTI ROCKS, DA, and SPIKE OF BENSONHURST. He is current Chief Operating Officer and Executive Producer of Apogee Productions.

High quality, independent films are the hardest to make, yet Grogg's ability, insight and skills demonstrated that independently produced films can be financed, distributed, and profitable. He shares the strategy behind FilmDallas, which was the financing entity for these films:

What was the original idea financing idea?

"FilmDallas Investment Fund I was a limited partnership formed as a venture capital investment fund targeted at the motion picture industry. The idea was to raise a blind pool of money without the investors having any real say or involvement in decisions regarding where to put the money or which movies to invest in."

157

What films were you trying to finance?

"None whatsoever. What we found there had been a lot of problems with raising money for motion picture production in Texas. This was the summer of '84 and there was an attitude and environment to put money into speculative ventures. 1984/85 was just the beginning of the sudden slide down that it still going down—the fortunes of those highly speculative ventures, like oil, gas, and real estate were diminished. But just prior to that the appetite was strong and it was possible to get venture capital into new areas whether it be high technology or, in our particular case, the motion picture industry. But the trick was to outline a plan based on investing not on making a particular film."

What did you tell these speculative investors you were going to do?

"First of all, we had been involved in a number of efforts to raise money for specific pictures. The traditional mechanism for raising private financing for movies was the limited partnership, which until the last few years had some limited tax advantages. In the 80's that changed and now there is really no tax or tax shelter advantage to using the limited partnership. But there is an advantage in limiting the investor's involvement in and the management of whatever the enterprise is and therefore limiting their liability."

"But mainly, from a producer's point of view, a limited partnership, if you're the general partner, your money becomes controllable in that it can not be involved in management without taking on liability. On the other hand, as a general partner in a limited partnership, you have general liability, and therefore you're in the cat's bird seat with all the cat bird's problems."

158

What did you tell your investors you were going to do and why did they invest with you?

"First, we analyzed other deals that were being promoted and we found that most investors in the private sector did not participate in these deals simply because they were not familiar with our industry— and our industry is a tough one to get to know because it's a club and its historically self-financed. This industry has been very reluctant to go into areas that other industries have traditionally used time and again for financing purposes. We only finance through a very select number of banks in the country and around the world that are specialists. We have taken stabs at raising money through Wall Street and investment houses. But raising money in the private sector for films—outside the industry—is a relatively new enterprise to this only 90 year old business. In the 1970's some of the first big stock offerings for movie production were launched. At that time, there were private investors who were interested in the motion picture industry but knew nothing about the decision process regarding what is a good investment, what is a bad investment, how do I control my investment, how do I maximize my potential for return? All those basic questions that you ask about any investment. They were difficult to answer, let alone understand on what basis to even start to formulate answers. The major decision was always, 'Which movie should I invest in?' In the FilmDallas scheme, the investor didn't decide what movie. The investor only decided on whether or not they wanted us to decide for them based upon our credentials, our track record, and what we articulate for them about how we will make the investment decision. The first thing we did is take the decision about the individual investments out of the investor's hands."

Kind of like a movie mutual fund. You were like the fund manager who picks the investments.

"Sure. It's like a mutual fund. I'm going to invest your money. And

159

then what we did in this particular instance is we said, now, we're going to take this fund and we're going to try to minimize the risk of your investment capital by diversifying it. We're not going to put it all on 'one horse.' So we will divide the fund up into chunks and we will limit the size and investments we can make in any one project. In simple terms we outlined specific criteria by which we would invest and manage those investments."

"We then further went on to articulate the kinds of things we would do and what we would not do and what we would endeavor to do, making sure that our investment took, if not <u>the</u> controlling position, a controlling position in any particular investment so that we had a say in how the project was managed. What that meant is that we didn't want to take too little of a piece so that we were just a minority player. At the same time, we made it clear that we wanted partners in all of our investments because we wanted somebody else to be on the hook in addition to us. We didn't want to be the total capital resource to make a movie because then what does the other side have to lose? So we said, for instance, that we would take no less than a 25 percent interest in any investment nor more than a 50 percent interest in any investment."

Did that give you creative approvals as well?

"Well that depends on the investment. Some of the investments we made were at the prints and ads level, but on the production investments, we sought and obtained approval over key elements just like a theatrical distributor who finances film production. The trick in order for us to get such approvals was we had to have legitimacy and credibility in the motion picture industry to be able to ask that. We had that."

"Today, sitting on the other side of the table from being an investor, if I seek private investment capital and if the investor isn't 'smart' or

160

intelligent about my industry, I tend to avoid making a deal. I think the worst thing you can do in raising money or financing this unique beast called motion picture production is to do it with dumb money. Ignorance will always rear its ugly head and bite you. Again, the limited partnership provides a bit of an advantage here because if you raise money through this vehicle your investor, assuming he or she has little understanding of the film business, can't get involved in the decision-making."

What was the size of the first fund?

"It was small. We had a lot of decisions to make at the beginning. We decided to get a deal done, so we lowered our sights, we raised $2-1/2 million. The structure was a limited partnership offering. $2-1/2 million minimum, $5 million maximum. We went out on the streets in the end of June 1984 and we closed the deal in 45 days, which was also a specific goal. We made a decision up front that if the deal didn't close fast, even though you're always promised if you just keep it open a few more days, there will be more money coming in, we would close it. And we did."

How many projects were you looking at?

"We did not have any specific goal. Actually, we invested in four or five projects over the period of a year and a half."

So you're talking about half a million dollars each?

"Yeah, roughly. We invested in a variety of ways but kept our participation at 25 percent to 50 percent of the total project cost in all cases."

Then it was a good time for low budget films because you had a burgeoning domestic and international video market that needed product.

161

"We were right there when the video explosion was happening, right before our eyes. But, I consciously made the decision, rightfully or wrongfully that what we had to do was establish, above all, our credibility which meant that a) I didn't want to lose money but b) I wanted to be involved creatively in the right kind of picture so I could begin to build off of a base to get access to the true upside element of movies which is the high-quality star/talent."

What were the first four pictures?

"CHOOSE ME, KISS OF THE SPIDER WOMAN, THE TRIP TO BOUNTIFUL and a little kid's movie called THE DIRT BIKE KID that we released theatrically in a very limited manner because it was a market niche we wanted to invest in—family entertainment."

"I told the investors we're going to be in modest-budget pictures with film makers who have proven track records. The only thing I said we wouldn't invest in is pornographic motion pictures or pictures that received ratings of "X.""

"So there were those limits. Nothing said we were couldn't invest in horror movies or teen exploitation movies. But I didn't want to put myself in a position, as a money raiser for production to start to try to explain why I thought one kind of motion picture, let alone a particular motion picture, had more chances for success than all those others out there. Because the fact of the matter is that most movies don't make money. And I put 'most' in capital letters.

What was your track record then?

"In that particular case, there were three of us, three general partners, myself, a lawyer and a banker. We had no prior experience in terms of investing in the motion picture industry. I had a lot of experience in terms of my knowledge of the motion picture industry and my connections within the motion picture industry, but I had never produced a movie, so I was a first-timer. And, in a way, it kind of worked for us. Because we said, we're going to study this industry and we're going to make studied and intelligent investments to the best of our ability and we explained at length the kinds of things we would look at and the kinds of controls we would absolutely require and the kinds we would endeavor to require and listed them in priority."

What are some of those things?

"Oh, nitpicky things—from wanting to see all of the pertinent contracts that relate to the production of the motion picture to asking about exclusivity of key elements and cross-collaterization of talents— whether or not the people who are investing in had other fish to fry somewhere else. We put together a four-page laundry list and, when I look at it now, it's all the questions that any producer of any movie, regardless of how it's funded asked themselves before, during and after the creation of a motion picture."

"You don't produce a movie unless you have some indication of the track records and abilities of your key players. You don't distribute a movie unless you've read the contracts. We clearly delineated that process and I remember talking to film makers who had been out on the streets trying to raise money for their films and they said, 'Wait a minute. If you guys are going to look at all this stuff, then I don't want any money from you,' and I said to one director/producer in particular, "What do you mean? Don't you have to, in the normal course of conducting your creative and business business, don't you have to know all that stuff?" We'll that's all I'm asking. I'm saying that in the course of our relationship, I'm going to make sure that all these things are examined and all these things are at least thought about."

Your primary concern here was to protect your investors.

"I think one of the tricks to raising money is to convince your
investors that you are articulate and knowledgeable in whatever it is
you're going to do. And the other thing is to know your limitations.
Too many times I've seen the filmmakers coming to me for money,
see, because I was in the position of an investor. I wouldn't only raise
the money. I also gave the money. And I've been in the position of
being a producer and in the position of being a distributor—I've sat in
all the chairs around the table that have to deal with this process of
putting money into and hopefully getting money out of a movie.
What I found was that too often the film makers were just that—
filmmakers. They weren't financial analysts, they weren't marketers,
they weren't salespeople, they were filmmakers and yet they found
themselves in this unenviable position of trying to explain to someone
who knew nothing about their business but who had money. And
they're trying to say, now, here's what we're going to do with your
money. And they can talk passionately about the film they're going to
make but they can't talk anything about how they're going to get
distribution. Well, we'll skip that, they say."

We'll go to film festivals they probably also say.

"Yeah, we'll just go to film festivals. My feeling is not that you have to
learn all that but what you should do is be ready for the investor's
kinds of questions and assemble around you a team that allows you to
say 'I don't know, but here's how we expect to get this answer.' If you
don't know the answer you need to be very articulate about the
process by which you will get the answer. That's how you protect
your investors."

What was the deal you offered your investors? How did that work?

"The basic deal was fairly typical. The limited partners' dollars came back into a pool, they received 99 cents of every dollar and the general partners received a penny."

The penny was to keep the business rolling on?

"Well, the investment capital that was raised allowed for a certain amount of it to go for the business—the operations of the investment fund. But we did some things that actually proved to be not so smart. Once the deal is capitalized, the first money that usually goes out is directly into the promoter of the deal's pocket to pay for all the development."

The development?

"The development. You know. All the American Express slips that he puts together over the years trying to beg people to give him money or whatever. What we were sensitive to is that we wanted to make sure our investors saw that we too were at risk. So, what we did is we budgeted what we felt our expenses would be on an annualized basis. We said we're gonna cap our expenses at this level. If they go over this, it will come out of our pocket. We, however, asked the partnership to allow us to do certain things, like consulting, to generate revenues to offset those expenses. We felt that we would have the time to generate all other kinds of fees because this movie investment business couldn't be that difficult once you pick and you bet your money. That's the end of it. So you just go off and wait for the checks to come in, right? Well, we found there was a lot more to the business of investing in the motion picture industry. Capping our expenses, it was a selling point of the deal at the time. It turned out that we didn't have the time to spend generating revenues to pay for our on-going expenses, the small staff and an office and everything, because we had to work our investments. Plus we were soon producing movies."

Did that mean you had to go back and amend the partnership?

"Yes. But what I guess I am saying is that when we packaged the deal, we were very investor sensitive. Almost to the point of our own fault. In terms of the relationship on the participation and income, until the investors recoup, they got 99 percent. After they recouped up to, I believe, two times their investment, it was 80/20 in their favor and then three times their investment, it was 60/40 and four times their investment, 50/50 and eventually it flipped at five times their investment to 40/60, 60 for the general partnership."

That was an extraordinarily rich deal for them.

"Very rich deal for the investor. That was again the climate and the idea behind it was if we were successful, it would all work out. The standard deal which I think is a little misconceived is that the investor's recoup their money and there's a 50/50 split. But that doesn't pay the investor for the time value of their money, their risk or anything."

Sometimes their payback is 120 percent before the general partners share.

"Sure, give them their payback plus some computed interest factor but you've got to calculate risk. You've got to understand that this isn't a CD. And even those are risky these days. That's not what it is. And I feel that to get investment capital out of private resources, you have to be sensitive to the fact that the investor can do other things that are safer, more controllable with their investment capital than invest it in motion pictures."

Did they get it back?

"It's still coming. As you might expect KISS and BOUNTIFUL will be returning revenues for quite awhile. I think that the expectation of their projected return is about 25 to 30 percent internalized rate of return. That means that it's discounted for present value."

People should be pretty happy with that.

"Yeah, but I don't think they're there yet because there is still money out of syndicated television, there's money that is in the pipeline from other revenue sources that just because of the nature of the industry, it hasn't come in yet."

What do these pictures do domestically?

"I think THE TRIP TO BOUNTIFUL did $6 or $7 million gross theatrical, shipped around 100,000 video units, then on and on. KISS OF THE SPIDER WOMAN did around 15 million domestic through reports have been as high as $18 and as low as $11 depending on whose counting. I think it did around $13 to $15 million domestically. and shipped around 110 to 120,000 video units. Island Pictures was the theatrical distributor. Embassy through Nelson was the video distributor."

"They were all real modest budget pictures. THE TRIP TO BOUNTIFUL probably was about $1.5 million, KISS OF THE SPIDER WOMAN was around $1.8 million, CHOOSE ME was $1.3 million."

"There was a window at that time for these specialty films that had opened up and the market became truly defined. The market was permanently put in place. It is still there today. There is a market for the more intelligent, more sophisticated, quality picture. Films like DRIVING MISS DAISY, MY LEFT FOOT, and other prove that the independent who created the base for such product did have an audience out there."

That's what the studios are doing now.

"That's exactly right. That's the point. And the smaller companies, those that are still in business, are having a much more difficult time simply because the studios are doing those kinds of pictures with Robin Williams and Kevin Costner, the big-time stars, which is cool. In the early '80's, DANCES WITH WOLVES would have never been made by a studio, but the independent might have taken the chance."

What's the financing strategy for today's producer?

"To be grossly simple, I think there's money in two arenas. In the United States the money is in the hands of the major studios and a couple of other independent distributors. That's who's financing the production of motion pictures. There's not money in Wall Street, except for Disney stock or something like that. There's not money in the private investment community that I can see."

Because?

"It's just that the economy is so ill-liquid and so conservative regarding investment that for me to say, 'hey, I think you can raise a substantial amount of money and by that I mean more than $500,000 to make a competitive motion picture,' I think is too hard. It's just a waste of time."

So, but what about the young player who wants to make his first movie?

"There's two things. I think its material-driven, strong material. A good idea well-executed will always be allowed to compete and just might win. The studios respond to material, screenplays, books and literary properties. Second, I still believe that extremely low-budget pictures that have a clear, distinct style hook or whatever, they can be made today and will be made tomorrow. The ROGER'S AND ME'S, the SEX, LIES AND VIDEOTAPES—they'll always come together. They will even be able to raise independent financing—there will always be someone out there who finally just can't say no to some obsessed film maker who won't let him say no."

And it's not because an investor sees the vision in the script or the property, because a lot of these things you won't know until the film got made.

"Sure, that's right. It's gonna continue to happen. One of the things that I find very interesting is that studios in the domestic scene are more open to the independent community. But that's a slightly more established independent community. Now in terms of other arenas, everybody says 'Go East young person to Europe' and all that. It's still difficult because there's been a lot of movement and a lot of changing and more supposed opportunity than real opportunity. If I'm a film financier in Budapest and I want to get into the movie industry, I want to get into it with Bruce Willis, I want to go do a deal with Hollywood, I don't want to do a deal with an independent film maker from The San Francisco Art Movement whose got this great docu-drama. The European community has always been very supportive of the artist. But the European film business is going to support its own artists and, when it comes to co-productions with the U.S. it will be for movies, not art."

But you were making art pictures!!

"Yes, I was. But I didn't initiate my discussions with my investors where I said anything about art. That was how I spent the money not how I got the money. I got the money by talking purely about investment in investor's terms and financial terms and certainly I disclosed that this was a creative endeavor and that there was a marketplace out there. But I went light on creativity, if you know what I mean."

169

You were an artist in a three-piece suit. You sneaked in there.

"That's absolutely right. But once I got in I tried not to abuse my welcome."

Now would that model work today? Did you ever do a FilmDallas II?

"No, what amounted to our FilmDallas II was raising the capital for FilmDallas, Inc. which then joined forces with New World Entertainment to form FilmDallas Pictures. And then that went the way of all flesh when the stock market crashed and the Texas banks crashed and the whole world crashed. The various components of that venture 1) the public company that had all this money in the stock market, and 2) the Texas banks that had all their money in FilmDallas, Inc. all crashed. On a go-forward basis, we had no way to stay afloat because our second round of financing—which we had always assumed would come from those sources became tapped out by forces that were much larger than anybody had any control over."

Could someone go out and make that kind of pitch today, the mutual fund model?

"Actually, I think that there's something to be said for the concept but there's also something to be said for the fact that young film makers should look to their peers as their financing sources. By that I mean, there's a new affluent young society. By young, I mean between the ages of 28 and 35 that are suddenly affluent and have disposable income and are very interested, as the whole world is, in the motion picture industry. We get young film makers who are just now graduating from UCLA or whatever, mid 20's, and they say, 'yeah, my friend went to Harvard and he's doing such and such. He's up in Silicon Valley and he's doing whatever' and you start talking to these young film makers and you say, 'Do you know how much money you know. You probably personally know more money than I knew when I walked into Dallas, Texas and started raising money.'"

"What young filmmakers should do is to appeal to the group which is their peer group. Don't try to go to some Donald Trump and expect him to invest in your little movie. Structure a deal which is articulate and (I hate to use this word) "hip" for people with whom you communicate regularly anyway. People to whom you have a connection."

"When we raised our initial capital, we literally cast our investors against the type of general partners we were. I did very little in terms of generating money. What I did is I explained how the movie industry works. It was like, bring me into the room, sit me down—I was the expert. I was fairly congenial, they liked me. I was non-threatening. But our banker and the lawyer who were wealthy themselves but also in the Texas business community—their presence in the deal and their molding of the deal so that it spoke to the concerns of their peers—was critical."

So, it was their peers.

"Right. All of us were in our late 30's, early 40's. Our investors were probably 40 to 50. And they were all putting in $50,000 dollars per unit."

That was the minimum per unit?

"One unit was 50 grand. And we did things that made it very easy for them. They didn't really put in cash. We arranged with a bank to take our investor's financial statements and, in essence, loan money to them at a predetermined, fairly favorable interest rate."

"They had a promissory note with the bank. The bank just gave us the money directly and then the investor had a choice regarding repayment. Either we paid the bank back or the investor back as the money came in. We arranged that financing for the investors so they could finance their participation in the deal."

Were you part of the approval process on the distribution contracts?

"Yes. We negotiated all the distribution contracts for the production investments."

Did you do okay with the negotiations because you had more than one picture?

"We did okay mainly because we looked like we were going to be a continuing source of financing."

Did you make the deals before film festivals or after them?

"It depended. Most of the distribution deals were made before the picture was made. Or sometimes a picture was in post-production and we invested in its distribution. KISS OF THE SPIDER WOMAN wasn't completed when we invested in the acquisition of the North American rights. CHOOSE ME was completed; we invested in both the distribution expenses as well as took a little equity piece in the picture. BOUNTIFUL we invested in the developmental stage where we, in essence, bought the rights to the play."

At what time were the distribution deals made?

"Well, with BOUNTIFUL we went out and made distribution deals coincident with production. Those were with Island domestic and then we made a foreign deal with J&M."

Tell me about the BOUNTIFUL foreign deal. Did you get an advance for the foreign deal?

"Yes. It was a $450,000 guarantee, all rights foreign. It was a very good deal for us. They wanted the picture a lot. We got educated real fast about how we negotiated our deals. We really sought the right kind of expertise and made an effort not to be stupid about it and, at the same time, recognized that we were newcomers."

"THE TRIP TO BOUNTIFUL , you have to remember is a movie about an old lady and a bus. To get a $450,000 advance guarantee, was no easy feat. I started looking for distribution on that movie before we started making it. The responses were like, 'well, you put up the expenses in advance for the foreign distribution and we'll consider doing it.'"

"That was kind of what PSO [Producer's Sales Organization, a foreign sales agent] told me. I didn't make the foreign deal until after I got the picture made. And as the picture was made and people began to see it was getting all this recognition, I began to change the deal. The domestic deal was $500,000 guarantee against all rights domestic with fairly conventional distribution fees. By the time I got the foreign deal, I had around $1 million total in guarantees."

Geraldine Page got the "Best Actress" Academy Award for The Trip to Bountiful?

"Right."

And Spider Woman?

"SPIDER WOMAN got Best Actor for William Hurt. It was nominated for Best Director, Best Picture, Best Screenplay Adaptation and Best Actress."

It can be done! Thank you, Sam Grogg.

THE ART AND
BUSINESS
OF LOW-BUDGET
FILMS

THE ART AND BUSINESS OF LOW-BUDGET FILMS

"What do you have that makes your project different from the other 30,000 projects that literally come across people's desks every year?"

Larry Kasanoff Interview

Larry Kasanoff worked with me for several years at Vestron, developing and acquiring special interest videos. He became Head of Lightning Pictures, Vestron's low-budget film division, where he oversaw the production of numerous films with budgets in the $1.5- to $3-million range, including DREAM A LITTLE DREAM. Later he was senior vice president of Vestron Pictures. From Vestron he went straight to the top and today he is an executive producer on TERMINATOR 2, one of the highest-budget films of all time.

We talked about low-budget films, which are entry level for most producers.

Today, who is making the $3-million-and-under movie?

"Two kinds of people. The occasional artsy film company-slash-art director, like Miramax with SEX, LIES, AND VIDEOTAPE, and the Roger Cormans. There used to be a zillion Roger Cormans around; now there's really just Roger and a few other people. The business has changed dramatically since the early home video days when the need for product to fuel a growing industry caused dozens of low-budget movies and companies to spring up. The home video industry matured, and it's become hit-driven like the book or theatrical movie business, driving a lot of low-budget film makers out of it."

177

There are thousands of producers out there who don't know that. Say you're a producer, the world's tough, you want to get $3 million. Let's map out what a strategy might be.

"Okay, but why are you using the number $3 million?"

I'm pulling it out of a hat.

"A slightly tough number these days."

Why?

"Because $3 million is in the middle. It's usually not enough money to give you star power, to attract a big company's interest. Yet it's too much for just a clever idea with a good hook. But $3 million or under $3 million, the principle is the same. Find a property and attach something interesting to that property to make it salable. That's what most people doing this for the first time don't understand. First, you need to have a great, high-concept idea with a special angle. What do you have that makes this project different from the other 30,000 projects that literally come across people's desks every year? Who cares that it's a good story and you've never directed a movie? That's not enough of an incentive to sell a low-budget movie unless you have an extraordinary, one-in-a-million script, which most people don't have. If you do, terrific, then you make SEX, LIES AND VIDEOTAPE because someone fell in love with your movie's idea. Second, it's easier if your story can be explained in half a sentence. I know that's not popular, but it's true. It's better if that half a sentence is the about the kind of movie that is popular around the world, meaning thriller, action, physical comedy. Every country in the world likes those movies. So, you take your high-concept idea with your special angle, and then you go and make a sale. You need to start pre-selling it. The best place to start is the foreign market."

All rights foreign?

"Yeah. All rights foreign. It's very difficult to split foreign rights in terms of splitting off video. So how do you sell foreign? You approach foreign sales companies that represent movies in the foreign markets with your high-concept idea, your special angle, and your script. You try to get a commitment from them for a money advance against the foreign rights to the film."

And they'll pay what?

"They'll say, 'We'll give you a million and a half dollars for all rights foreign as an advance and sell the movie for you all over the country. We'll take a commission, a sales agency's fee, for selling it. We'll pay you when you deliver.'"

Like what, 25 percent, 30 percent?

"Yeah, more like 30 percent. You can negotiate down at times, too, depending on the strength of your project, down to as low as 15 percent."

So it's like a pickup. They'll guarantee an advance upon delivery.

"Right, and then they'll go out and sell it."

What do you need to go to them? Do you need a trailer? Do you need a script? Do you need to have it cast?

"You need a script and almost always an element to it. You need to have a cast. You say to them, 'Look, if I can deliver this script with a famous actor in it, what will you give me for it?' And then they'll tell you. They'll give you an advance only if you have a famous actor in it. The question is, how do you do that, because you can't go to a famous actor and just chat with him, unless he happens to be your best friend. It's a chicken-and-egg situation."

"Sometimes producers don't have exactly the talent they claim they do or maybe they've just begun tentative conversations and are fishing. But this is the only way they can get the ears of the talent's agent and the sales rep. It's frustrating because one will never commit before the other. So you end up saying the same thing to both: 'Stay right here; hold on; I'll be right back.'"

"Right. How do you keep the talent still while you're raising money for your project? That's the most difficult thing."

How do you do it?

"There's no easy way. You just have to be absolutely relentless. Never be dishonest but be creative."

So you have to build confidence on each side that it's not going to fall apart and no one will be embarrassed.

"Absolutely. And it always falls apart. What you try then is going to these sales companies to get preapproved lists: 'What if I can get one of these five people?' 'Okay, any of these five people, we'll give you a million and a half dollars for all rights foreign.' You can do it that way to give yourself some leeway. Now, you should be relatively familiar with those five people before you do it. Nothing destroys a buyer's confidence quicker, in my opinion, than your reeling names off the top of your head, completely fabricating. You want to have talked to the talent agents. A good buyer will know if you're lying. He'll call the talent's representation. And if they say they've never heard of the seller, forget it. They won't even take your phone calls anymore."

Let's talk about the psychology, the attitude that you have to wear in order to be successful.

"That's goes back to the earlier question: 'Why is $3 million your first time out a hard number?' Because it is a significant amount of money to raise."

Well, give me some other strategies. Maybe there's a $250,000 strategy and an $8 million strategy.

"Let's say you want to make a movie for $800,000 because you want to get into the movie business. You come up with a fabulous concept, and you might invest in a piece of key art yourself, because with $800,000 you must be able to get the movie made without a star."

So, what's the concept? Hot Dog: the movie?

"Yeah, this is HOT DOG: THE MOVIE, so you hire an artist to draw the key art. One strategy to get well-known names is to find actors who will do one or two days of shooting cameos in your film. (You might have one name actor who appears throughout the film, and other cameos to elevate your marquee and advertising.) You might pay from $15,000 to $20,000 for a day, and send a limo for them. A lot of older actors might like this. If you get them to do something they normally wouldn't do they might like it even more. Be sure the deal includes using their name on the ads and publicity. Then you can go to the foreign sales agent and say you've got whomever.

"You have to be able to get more on the screen for a little money because you're trying to increase the film's perceived value so your foreign sales rep can sell it for more. The real trick is to bring in more dollars in advances than the budget calls for so you're profitable before you shoot.

"When the sales agents go to the festival, ask to go along to learn the business.

181

"Another way to make a film look like more is to get a good writer to write cheap and motivate him to do 17 rewrites. Then find a great production manager who gets locations cheaper than anyone else. Use the Roger Corman low-budget approach. Design your project, for example, around a hotel. You can get a luxury hotel for nothing during off season. Or find a set you can use after someone else has finished with it."

You don't ever move anybody; you stay in one place.

"You stay in one place. You write the script to do that. And you try to get terrifically talented people. How do you do that? Usually by giving people who haven't done it before a shot. Your second A.D. becomes your first A.D. because no one else will let him be first A.D. at this stage in his career. Your production auditor becomes your production manager, because no one else would want to be production manager. Your assistant art director becomes your art director. Your assistant editor becomes your editor. You find young people with talent and you take a shot with them. One of your jobs as a producer is to spot undiscovered talent."

You are looking for people who've done the work before under the auspices of someone else.

"Exactly. That's why these movies are sometimes so horrible and sometimes gems. You're not hiring a $9,000-a-week director of photography. You're hiring a gaffer or an ex–film student who'd love to do it. And you're doing that all day long. Also, in this world there are veteran low-budget people, and you might want to hire one or two of them to make sure you know what you're doing."

You do that by looking at other low-budget movies.

"Right. If one is going to be in this business, one should be extraordinarily familiar with movies, every movie. In fact, when I started working for you, Michael, I took home a movie every night for a year until I had seen Vestron's entire library. You watch everything, you find out who did it, you find out how much they made it for, and you get to the point where you can look at a movie and try and figure out how much it was made for. And you start investigating foreign deals in foreign countries. What if I go to Argentina? Where can I get different locations at a lower price? Where can I get people to give me deals?"

Where do you put most of your money? Not in the talent, not in the people, but in the actors and the script?

"Well, in a low-budget movie you're pretty much paying all the actors SAG minimum. By the way, in my opinion one should never make a non-SAG movie."

Because you need experienced actors.

"Non-SAG would be so hard to do and so hard to find. Non-SAG movies are generally so horrible that your film wouldn't be taken seriously. There are a lot of good people in SAG, and SAG minimum is affordable in these budgets. And there's a special low-budget SAG category. Plus, you want to establish relationships with talent."

So you put the money in the actors and the script?

"No, because again the actors are already low."

What'll it cost for an $800,000 movie, $30,000 or $40,000?

"Yeah, you shouldn't be spending more than $40,000 on the script.

183

But if you do, though, that would be okay because almost every penny is going on the screen. You don't have a lot of money, no one gets a trailer."

You pay for your production manager—he's the key—and your cinematographer, I imagine.

"You pay for your production manager. Your cinematographer is a luxury you try to pay for because he makes movie look good, but then you don't have a hell of a lot of money. Then you've got to get a great editor."

What about music? With the great number of hungry composers around you shouldn't have any trouble finding quality work.

"Music you can find. I've paid $200,000 for scores in my $10-million movies, and I've paid $25,000 for scores in my million-dollar movies, and there's not necessarily a direct correlation. Besides being a master organizer, you must be able to spot talent of all kinds. How do you find a $25,000 composer? How do you get a composer who works for $75,000 to score your movie for $25,000? How do you get him or her excited about your idea? By being a complete salesman all the time."

Let's swing it back to financing. Let's do the $800,000 model. Can you really go to a foreign sales agent and expect to pick up a few hundred thousand dollars?

"What you're trying to do is get $800,000; you're trying to get your movie financed. And how are you doing that?"

By making it look and sound like a $3 million movie.

"And giving your potential buyers what they want so they in turn can sell it. Yeah, you're trying to sell them on the fact that it's going to look like a $3 million movie. You're saying, 'Look, it's a great idea and I've got these two cameos. You're going to make this much money; what do you care what my budget is?' You try and play that game, at which you will be only moderately successful.

"Vestron tried to overpackage movies and get from 75 to 90 percent of the movie financed from foreign sales. DREAM A LITTLE DREAM had Jason Robards, Corey Haim, Corey Feldman, Harry Dean Stanton, Victoria Jackson, and Alex Rocco. It also had a soundtrack that won a gold record; and it was made for a little over $3 million. Corey and Corey had been in three hit movies; they're huge teen stars.

"Vestron also made a million-dollar movie with Charles Grodin, Sally Kellerman, Kristy McNichol, and David Leisure. They all played cameos, but the cameos lasted from 10 to 15 minutes each because of the way they were cut. The movie was populated with terrific people. The producer represented some. The director was friends with the stars. Charles Grodin had complete freedom to do whatever he wanted. We gave a tremendous amount of leeway. No points were given to the actors."

Are the big movies taking all the presell money out of the market?

"To a large extent, yes. The B movie business is extremely difficult."

Is that going to come back?

"I believe it will—although not the way it was a few years ago—because eventually the pendulum swings. It swung to the extreme overproduction side when video was growing, and now it will swing in the opposite direction. Movie production is down 35 percent this year.

It's going to be down next year."

*How many independent pictures will be made this year? A hundred? A
hundred fifty?*

"About 200 independent movies and 200 major films get made in the
United States every year. To qualify for the Academy Awards, a film
has to be released in Los Angeles in a commercial movie theater for
seven days continuously. Interestingly enough, only 217 movies, less
than the year before, qualified for Academy Awards this year."

So only half the movies found screens.

"In Los Angeles. That doesn't mean they weren't on someplace else.
But of the thousands and thousands of scripts offered each year, only a
few hundred are produced.

"Vestron, a medium size company, saw 7,000 scripts a year. The
industry probably saw 30, 40, 50 thousand, who knows? The game is
having either an extraordinarily good script or a script that talent finds
so terrifically exciting you can book them."

You've got to get to know the talent agents that know the actors.

"Yeah. You've got to take shots. You've got to get good at reading the
trades, reading every magazine, going to every movie. You've got to be
able to make a YOU CAN'T HURRY LOVE with the right kind of
talent and a good soundtrack for a million dollars. Look at the numbers.
All you do as a buyer is eliminate all day long, looking for the one or
two little gems. I could make ten movies a year from the 7,000 scripts
I got, and five of those would be from ideas we sat around and thought
up ourselves. So out of those 7,000 scripts, five a year would get bought
and turned into a movie. And you could eliminate 5,000 scripts on
just..."

...what the cover page looked like.

"Yeah. And then it's important how to pick projects, how to sell projects, know what buyers want. Right after DIRTY DANCING came out I got a phone call from someone who had a script about a gorgeous young virgin in a nunnery who goes crazy and kills the other thirteen beautiful young girls. And I explained that that's not exactly the kind of programming we're looking for, and he said, 'I don't understand. It's just like DIRTY DANCING. It's "innocence loses its innocence." Don't you see?' You want to be pitching something that makes sense. You want to be to the point, enthusiastic, short, targeted, and focused."

So you encourage people to go more towards traditional genre pictures than art movies.

"I encourage people who want to make movies to do so. Play to your strengths. There's no right or wrong. Pursue your possibilities, but be aware of what the market wants.

"Hemdale as a producer has an intriguing strategy, making interesting, quirky movies because of their appeal to a lot of actors who want good roles. Hemdale gets movies produced for a fraction of what others pay because they let people star—and direct—these movies. They pre-sell the foreign rights for an amount greater than the normal percentage because they overpackage the movie relative to its price. Budgets are in the $3- to $6-million range.

"The big point is that you have to have an angle on what separates you from the masses, whether that angle is simply that I have HOT DOG: THE MOVIE and it's a great idea and a blast and now's the right time for it, or that I have the best art-actor script in the world. Play to your stengths.

"When you sell a buyer, you want him to say, 'Boy, I can sell that.' You need something that distinguishes you. You can always go to the independent companies and try to get one to produce your movie, but there are few independent companies left now."

Let's talk about that for a minute. Any smart investor's not going to be interested unless you can guarantee distribution. How would you model a limited partnership strategy?

"It's very difficult to convince people that you have a good idea and they should invest in it. People invest for two reasons: because they are interested in the movie business, and because it's fun. For someone who's worth $40 million and made all his money in steel drilling bits, maybe spending $25,000 in a partnership might be a fun thing to do. It's like buying a lottery ticket, there are enough cases of a huge upside."

So you're going to go sell 35 shares at $25,000 each and make an $800,000 movie?

"Yeah, you can try it that way. Boy, it's hard. I wouldn't recommend it."

Then how are you going to get distribution?

"Now you're in a different ball game. You've made your movie and you're taking a shot. A very hit-or-miss business."

And you go the film festival route if you've got an art or drama or comedy that they'll like. But what about genre pictures that won't play in festivals?

"They're not the festival route, they're the shopping route. When your movie gets finished, no one asks if you spent $10 million on it or a dollar on it. I mean, they ask you, but they don't care. Because it's

188

worth what it's worth. Warner Bros. bought STAND AND DELIVER for $5 million, and the movie was made for about a million. I'm guessing at these numbers. That's why it's a hit-or-miss business. When you're done with your $800,000 movie, you're going to call up every distributor and say to the acquisitions person—you would have already told them you were making the movie, so they know who you are—'My movie's finished. I would like you to look at it.' And they will; that's their job."

What's a strategy to create interest in the film?

"You want to try to convince A that B loves it and B that C loves it and so on. But when they look at your $800,000 movie, if they don't like it, they're going to give you zero for it. They don't want it anymore. If they love it, if two people love it, you might sell it for $2 million."

It's creating the perception that they love it, which may not have anything to do with the movie.

"Well, on a finished film it's much harder to create a buzz than it is on a script. Because in the buzz business, you're always better off selling the sizzle; you're always going out selling the possibility. The finished movie sits there. People look at it. What you can do with buzz on a finished movie, if people like it, is bid up the price. But you can't convince people who don't like it to like it."

What about selling your investors and distributors from a trailer?

"Then you have to raise the money to go shoot a trailer. I think it's a very dangerous business to be in, because when someone showed me the trailer I have been turned off on many projects that I sort of liked."

You feel differently about art work.

"If you can't make a great piece of key art, don't do it. Charlie Band, who used to run a company called Empire that Vestron bought from extensively, was a master. Charlie created the most intriguing sci-fi movie key art. He would come to Vestron twice a year and we'd go through key art. At that time, the video business was so strong we knew that if we picked the right key art at the right price we'd at least break even, and if the movie was good we'd make a lot of money. Charlie financed his entire company through creating key art for Vestron for three years. But that business is largely over. It's very difficult. The kind of people who are getting these independent movies made now are getting them cast well."

Say, you want to make movies at the $8 million level. What will that buy you?

"At $8 million you can start to make a movie that I call 'with no excuses.' While a studio would make that movie for $12 million; nonetheless, you can still make that movie and say, 'This movie may be good or bad, but I can't blame it on the money. I'm no longer in the "Well, if I only had more money business."' We spent $10 million on BLUE STEEL, which was shot for nine weeks in Manhattan with Jamie Lee Curtis and Ron Silver. It's an action movie. Oliver Stone and Ed Pressman produced the film, I executive-produced it and we had an extraordinary line producer. It looks gorgeous. I mean, I love the movie. We didn't lack anything in that movie."

You had everything you needed: enough time, enough talent.

"We bought the movie out at a turnaround. The studios had budgeted it at from 20 to 40 percent more than we did. BLUE STEEL had been set to go in Chicago at, I believe, $14 million. When I got involved, I said we could make it for $10 million, and in New York.

They all thought I was completely crazy: New York is the most expensive city in the world; we couldn't possibly do that. Well, we switched the Chicago line producer, who wasn't familiar with New York, and we got involved with Mike Rauscher, who was co-producer on the movie and terrific, and we shot the movie in New York. I mean, I've shot a movie for a million dollars in New York. It's a great place to work, but you have to know how to work there. We got the Gold Exchange to let us shoot during active trading—no one has ever gotten them to do that before in the history of film—and we get this beautiful, huge shot with 3,000 extras trading on the exchange for free."

Why'd they do it?

"Because they loved the script. Because of the people associated with it—Oliver, Ed, Kathryn."

This was post–Wall Street?

"This was post–*Wall Street*. The producer told them that Vestron went out on the line and moved this movie away from Chicago to their backyard, to Manhattan. We brought $10 million worth of business into New York so they did it for us. They shut down one street on Wall Street for the day, which they'd also never done. So you have to start doing things like that, play that game, look at things in a different way from other people. At a time when everyone was running from New York, we ran right to it. At the $10 million budget range you can really start to make it terrific. You can make terrific movies at all ranges, but it's still hard. People are still working 12-hour days. It's an amazing feat, but you can do it."

What resources and connections with other people will you need if you are just starting out as a producer? Most people aren't going to arrive in Hollywood with the experience that you have. What do you need and how do you get it?

"The best thing to do is throw yourself in the middle of it. I believe you have to be in a filmmaking center to do this, which is basically Los Angeles, although to an extent you can get away with New York. And you need to know people. You need to know line producers, DPs, editors, writers, agents. It's not hard to meet them. How? People are very open. You call them up. You say, 'Hey, I just rented your movie, Mr. Line Producer; it's terrific. Can I buy you lunch?' And Mr. Line Producer will be delighted to do lunch."

The producer probably won't go to lunch with you.

"You don't walk into town from Minneapolis and call the head of a studio, but you certainly walk into town from Minneapolis and call the co-producer of a low–budget movie and say, 'Hey, I really liked your film. Could I meet you. I have an idea.' Be persistent. I've hired directors on some of my bigger movies who've directed one movie that was not particularly successful, although I thought it showed terrific work. I've done that at all levels. I've hired people who've made $2 million movies to make $10 million movies; but I've also hired people who've made $300,000 movies to make $2 million movies. The resources you need are knowing people, and you just have to start meeting them. The other important thing, I think, is to get involved. When you're in the movie business and the TV business, if you're an actor you should be acting, if you're a writer, you should be writing, and if you're a producer, you should be producing. Work on something. Just get into it. And your contacts will increase exponentially."

What about lawyers and agents?

"You should always have a terrific lawyer."

And how do you find one? Say you've just moved here from Minneapolis.

"You just start asking people. I think people in any business should have a good lawyer. Agents? Should you have an agent as a producer? It depends. That's a hard call."

An agent's not going to do something unless you already have a deal happenning.

"Yeah, today, to be a producer without a deal at a studio is extraordinarily difficult. It's more difficult to be an independent producer today than it has been in 10 or 15 years. I don't necessarily believe that's going to be true two years from now."

Because of what's happened in home video? Because there are too many players?

"Yeah, because all these independent companies are going out of business, production is down, and it's the era of the big, huge movie. If you look at the movie business over many years, there's rarely been a time when independent movies aren't present. So one thinks they have to come back. Plus, there's been an abundance of movie screens built over the last couple of years. When you look at the economics of more screens and fewer movies, it seems independent movies have to come back."

I believe independent films pulled in about 5 percent of the gross box office a few years ago, and now I think it's down to about 3 percent.

"I don't know that number. It's really shocking. Yet, the other important thing to remember when you walk into town from Minneapolis is you don't have to make *Batman* as your first movie. Making a solid movie and treating everyone right and paying your bills, and making a solid $800,000 movie that maybe gets released—but maybe it doesn't;

maybe it sells a lot of videocassettes and enjoys a nice run on HBO—that's an okay thing to do. At least you're making movies, and that's what you should be doing."

Have you worked with any banks on small pictures?

"Several."

Who will make loans to small pictures?

"A lot less today than before."

And how does it work?

"Again, that's back to your presale business. What happens, you've now been successful. You've gone to a foreign sales company and gotten a $500,000 guarantee. And you've gone to a domestic video company that just for the heck of it has bought all rights domestic from you because maybe they'll get it released for you. And they paid you $600,000. Now you have paper that says when you deliver this movie based on this script, they're going to give you, respectively, for the movie and script, $500,000 and $600,000. You first go to a completion bond company. A completion bond company insures that the movie will get finished on budget."

Such as?

"The Completion Bond Company."

Will they do low-budget movies?

"Yeah, they will, and they're absolutely terrific. They're the people

I've used. I've made 25 movies with them and they're terrific. There are others, too, but I'm not as familiar with them. You can't get a loan without a completion bond, by the way. The bank will require that."

If I were going to pay that kind of money, I'd want to have approvals over the picture during production.

"They will have approval over everything before the picture starts. It's a huge bureaucratic nightmare. A bank closing, you have to sign every page of the script, you have to sign everything. Any element that you change, you have to change with these distributors. And then the bank cares only what the distributor will accept. They don't per se care, but if the distributor specifies these five cast members, this director, this script, and this location, the bank is going to make sure you do all of them."

So if you shoot something extra, you can't put it in, and you can't cut something out without approval?

"That gets technical. Things get changed and edited and so forth and, again, you want to be dealing with people who are in the business. If one is a buyer, one isn't in the business of trying to screw the bank. So if on page 70 you changed a line from 'He crosses the room and smashes a glass' to 'He sits down and looks furtively,' that's okay. Changes have to be material changes. If you say that a famous actor is in the movie and it turns out that the famous actor's brother-in-law is in the movie not the famous actor, that's a different story.

"Then you take your paper from reputable people, you go to the completion bond company, which says to the bank, 'Yes, we will guarantee this movie.' And for a percentage of the movie they will do that."

How much?

"Initially 5 or 6 percent. You can get better deals once you're a bigger client. Then you go to the bank. You say, 'I have two contracts from very reputable companies,' which the banks are going to check, and 'I have a bond with a completion bond company.' Before they sign off, the banks will see every piece of paper you have: 'Let me see your talent contracts,' 'Let me see your writer contracts.' You have to be so in order to do this, and it takes a long time. Remember, the bank is going to discount you because they make an interest payment. So you have a million one, by the time the bank's through with you, you don't have a million one anymore, because you're paying the banks a lot of money. How much is that? Depending on the bank, 10, 15, 20 percent."

So the discount pays the interest.

"Sure."

So basically, it's like 900,000 and they make another $100,000 or whatever it is.

"Yeah. It's like someone says to you, "Michael, I'll give you a million dollars two years from now." They don't give you a million dollars; they give you its present value. And that's what the bank is doing. Because you're saying to the bank, 'I've got a million dollars two years from now,' or a million one, and they're saying, 'Great, but today it's worth this, because I'm making interest on it.' And that's what they do.

"Now, which banks? It depends. Wells Fargo, Bank of America, Credit Lyonnais. Credit Lyonnais used to be huge in it; not so much now. There's a French bank called Credit du Nord that's doing it. British and Commonwealth. These are all foreign banks that are very active. First Bank of Minnesota, I believe, or Minneapolis, is very active. Security Pacific was for a while; Chemical Bank was for a while. They all have entertainment lending divisions in Los Angeles. If you have a bond from a completion bond company and your distribution contracts are from reputable people, generally speaking, you can get your contract banked."

I would think that small, one-picture companies would scare them.

"The completion bond only guarantees that the movie gets finished.

"The completion bond tells the bank that the movie's going to get finished for a million one. The bank is concerned about two things, can you do it on budget, and the completion bond covers that, and two, once you're done, having done it on budget, are these companies going to pay you? Because what if it's Frank's Foreign Distributors and they have no assets and you give them the movie and they say, 'Gosh, gee, I know we promised you $600,000, but we had a bad year.' So your distributors have to be creditworthy and you have to have a completion bond. God forbid a completion bond company ever takes over your movie; it's the worst thing in the world to happen, because they will then technically fulfill the script, but they won't care about the creative quality of it; nor should they, because you've screwed up. So that becomes a mess. The whole thing is very complicated."

Is it worth doing on a low-budget picture? Five percent of a picture is a lot of money if you're talking about only $800,000.

"You can't get your movie financed through a bank if you don't have it. It simply can't be done."

Then maybe you can't do it that way. Maybe you have to go to investors?

"But if you don't do that, you can't presell your movie. Any investor with any brains won't do it without a completion bond either. So is it worth it? Well, is it worth having earthquake insurance? Is it worth having insurance on anything? Relatively speaking, there's insurance for all kinds of extraordinary causes. How many people have cranes fall on their houses? Not many, but still you would want to have insurance on your house. I think it's worth it."

You had insurance on all your low-budget pictures because it was Vestron's corporate imperative.

"Well, that's actually not true, because I was given carte blanche not to do it after the first few movies but I always did. And I never called in the bond. I wound up getting a very good deal because I gave them so much business. As a producer you're hiring dozens and dozens of people to make a movie. You are an employer, so you have to have workman's compensation and you have all kinds of insurance like any other kind of employer.

"Is all of it worth it? Friends outside the business say to me, 'I don't get it. Two years to make a movie?' It's from start to finish about a zillion moving parts, from the idea through to getting the movie released in the right theaters, and you just have to be on them all day long, and that's what you do as a producer."

Thank you, Larry Kasanoff.

SUCCESS

IN

HOME VIDEO

SUCCESS IN HOME VIDEO

"The standard contract is the contract that a distributor would like you to sign."

Success in Home Video

Success in home video is defined by the number of units sold. A major studio film sells from 300,000 to 700,000 units through video rental stores at retail prices ranging from $59 to $99. A low sell-through pricing of $29 and under for a video might sell one to three million tapes. An independently produced film does very well if it sells 150,000 units. Original, special-interest programs selling over 50,000 units are considered hits.

Some home video companies like RCA, Warner, SONY, Virgin, LIVE, and MEDIA produce films that go directly to home video without a theatrical release. Most of these have strong exploitation elements and are clearly genre films. While video retailers have greatly reduced their purchases of "B" titles, the right promotable elements still result in successful "B" movies. Unless a producer looks to television and foreign sales, a domestic-only direct-to-video film budget is generally below $250,000.

There is no cookie-cutter formula for successful home video programs, but some elements elevate a video's chance for financial returns by making the program more attractive to investors and distributors alike. Ask yourself the following questions:

1. *Is my cast as strong as possible?*
Look for talent like Mickey Rourke and Michael Caine who have a strong following among video renters. Carry this criterion over into the foreign markets, but make sure your cast appeals to other

201

territories and cultures if you expect to make foreign sales. Consider that your cast may have to pass approval by financial entities.

2. Do I have a recognizable director?

Directors, to a greater degree than before, are being recognized by the home video audience.

3. What is the genre?

Although video stores are filled with horror and violence, comedy and family films are making a comeback.

4. Was the film (or video) released with sufficient publicity and advertising to generate awareness?

Word of mouth on a video title begins with the theatrical release, so the stronger the theatrical release the better.

5. Is my budget appropriate in scale to the genre I am producing?

Each film or video has a potential that is based on its genre. Don't overspend on those genres in which greater expenditures may not bring in more profits. Underspending can be problematic for genres that need a quality look or expensive elements. The real issue is anticipated profitability. Financiers and distributors will look at a film or video based on its "upside." The greater the upside, the greater the desire on the investor or distributor's part.

Most foreign films, for example, have limited earning potential, except for an occasional breakthrough hit like MY LIFE AS A HOUND. Even then, earning potential is still limited in comparison with other genres. Distributors are only equipped to promote, release, and distribute so many films a year and must justify their projected earnings for each film launched. Producers often think that investors will get their money back faster if a film is low budget. What they don't realize is the high cost and risk of marketing the film and the value of a distributor's release slot. A distributor will not invest much

P&A money on a film that—because of its low budget—has no cast or production quality, or is a genre with little upside.

6. *What is the quality of the film or video? Does the quality meet the expectations of its audience? Will the quality of the film contribute to its success in its market?*

7. *What are the business elements? Is there any equity financing already in place? Any rights been pre-sold? Are there domestic and/or foreign co-production partners? What rights are still available?*

8. *Is the scale of the film or video large or small? Are locations a primary element?*

9. *Is there a strong script or story?*

10. *Is the producer reputable? Director? Director of photography? Composer?*

The Home Video Deal

If you are making a film, the home video rights will probably end up with the theatrical film distributor. If you are making a film that is going direct-to-video without a theatrical distributor, or you have an original, non-theatrical video, or a film that will not find a foreign theatrical distributor, you may deal directly with a home video manufacturer. (Home video distributors are called *"manufacturers"* or *"suppliers."* The manufacturers produce or acquire video product and sell it to *"distributors"* [or wholesalers] who in turn sell it to video *"retailers."* The producers most frequently make their deals with manufacturers.)

Your first order of business is to assess the objectives of each home video company and the kind of films (or videos) it acquires. What does their existing library look like? What does their upcoming release slate look like? Who buys upfront and what do they pay? Like any other research project, this requires due diligence on the producer's part. He will want to learn everything he can from agents, lawyers, sales agents, and other producers who have dealt with the prospective video companies. Producers who have contracts with these manufacturers may be willing to share their distribution contracts with you so that you can have a idea of the deal terms. They may let you know the areas in which the manufacturer backed away from points in the *"standard contract."*

By the way, **there is no such thing as a standard distribution contract.** I know what manufacturers say about their own contracts: *"Oh, it's the same deal we have with all of our producers."* Not so. Every film or video is different. Every deal is different. When I worked for Vestron I acquired or commissioned (sometimes both) over 200 videos for production. They were all different in one way or another.

The standard contract is the contract that a manufacturer would like you to sign; it is not necessarily the contract that you would like to sign. It's all negotiable. The final contract is a reflection of how good your negotiation skills are and how valuable your program appears to the buyer. The marketplace will determine the price. If you push too far, you'll get a "no." If they push too far, you'll retort with a "no" (if you're confident you can get a better deal elsewhere). Another factor that can affect your deal is the climate and health of the marketplace and your video's potential.

In rare instances when you do business with a small independent distributor that **isn't attached** to a home video company, you look for an advance against royalties, or a guarantee, or a production advance.

You usually obtain an **advance against royalties** after a film or video is finished. The quality of the film is known. The marketplace may or may not bid on the program. The advance (and royalty) are probably the two determining factors in what deal you take (but not necessarily —there's fine print to read)!

A *guarantee* means that the video manufacturer will guarantee you some income, usually over a period of time. A proportion of the agreed-upon guarantee can be paid upon signing, upon release, sixty days after release, six months after release, three years after release, or any combination of these. The manufacturer is trying to stretch out the cash flow and his payment schedule to you. A guarantee gives him the opportunity to collect money before paying you.

A *production advance* is what you may be looking for in order to produce your film or video. The terms are usually the toughest because the distributor hasn't seen the finished product and is betting with you that it will be good (or at least worth the money being put up). If the distributor takes a risk like this you can bet the deal will be tougher than if you have a finished picture.

Usually the production advance is paid out during the course of production. It wouldn't be unusual for the manufacturer to have approvals at various stages and release monies at the approval points. A payment schedule for a video might be the following: one fifth upon signing, one fifth upon completion of principal photography, one fifth upon rough cut approval, one fifth upon fine cut approval, and one fifth upon delivery. In this case the producer works out the production cash flow and hopes that the payment schedule coincides with the bills as they fall due. If there is a shortfall the producer may have to go to the bank or get financing from other sources.

For a feature, it's now reasonably standard for a video manufacturer to look to the scale of the theatrical print and advertising commitment when determining an advance or guarantee. As mentioned before, it's hard to do business without a P&A commitment. (If you are making a film that goes direct-to-video, the assessment will be a simple calculation of how many videos the manufacturer thinks he can sell. A made-for-video feature that sells 5,000 copies yields about $75,000 in royalties from $250,000 in gross home video revenues.)

Distributors try to wait until your film is completed before making a deal, unless they feel the film is really hot or that their competitors might beat them to the punch. Naturally the producer will try to get as much "buzz" going about the feature before showing it to distributors in order to raise the price. Remember, it's a game. A financial game, and the stakes are everyone's money.

The worst situation is to finish your film and find it's not very good. Or to finish it and find your distributor has a cash flow problem and can't meet his commitment to you. Or to have the distributor try to renegotiate a lower P&A commitment that can possibly blow your home video deal. That's assuming, of course, that you are negotiating with both a theatrical distributor and a home video manufacturer, which is unlikely.

More likely is a theatrical distributor that has either his own video distribution company or an output relationship with a home video company. He wants to control both the theatrical and home video rights.

Split Rights

Think of your film or video as a property made up of various rights that can be bundled together or broken apart for selling. You can go either to one distributor, who will in turn work with various subdistributors to exploit the rights in your property, or you can go to a variety of distributors, each specializing in a particular set of rights (foreign television, non-theatrical, etc.).

Until recently, producers were able to split their rights up and make deals with a number of distributors. A producer might receive one advance from a U.S. theatrical distributor and another from a U.S. home video company and repeat this scenario in various territories throughout the world. By parceling out the rights in this fashion, he could raise more than the production cost of the film and be into profits even before it was shot.

Theatrical distributors quickly learned that home video revenues were in effect a result of their advertising expenditures and publicity efforts. Since they paid for the film's exposure and risked their own cash, they began to demand participation in revenues downstream. Today, to protect their downside, theatrical distributors no longer only acquire theatrical rights but insist on home video (and sometimes foreign) rights as well. The greater the investment by the theatrical distributor, the greater the demand for more rights.

Producers are no longer able to split or "splinter" rights, although big name action sequels may be the only exception. From time to time you may hear about deals in which splintering did occur, such as the SEX, LIES, AND VIDEOTAPE deal discussed above in which Miramax owns the North American theatrical and television rights and RCA/Columbia the video rights and Virgin the foreign rights. But today this is extremely rare.

Nevertheless, a producer should still examine his property and be aware of the value of the rights when making a financing/distribution deal. The rights in many films include the following:

> Theatrical Rights
> Non-Theatrical Rights
> Home Video Rights
> Television Rights
> Novelization Rights

Sound Track Rights
Merchandising Rights

Foreign Theatrical Rights
Foriegn Non-Theatrical Rights
Foreign Home Video Rights
Foreign Television and Cable Rights
Foreign Novelization Rights
Foreign Sound Track Rights
Foreign Merchandising Rights

Promotable Elements

A video manufacturer looks for the very same promotable elements in your film as a theatrical distributor does: stars (this appeals to the home video market), a strong salable genre (action and comedy over drama or art), a large P&A commitment from a strong theatrical distributor, a good story, a strong script, an established producer, director, and director of photography, and foreign potential.

The Distribution Dilemma

As we've previously discussed, financing your project with a pre-sale reduces your upside. If the film is great, it's possible to create a bidding war with theatrical distributors that will increase your P&A deal and improve your home video advance. If the film is poor, you are really in trouble. Any investors will probably lose their money.

The problem with the business of distribution is that you have two or three parties with different goals. Each has a self-serving interest that does not necessarily benefit the film or one another.

The **producer's goal** is to get cash from as many revenue streams as possible. This suggests splintering rights, which is very difficult. He tries to protect his investor's upside (and his own) but this may mean finishing his film without a distributor, which is risky. In order for home video sales to be strong, a distributor has to commit to a certain level of P&A. It's not uncommon for distributors to change their commitments for a variety of reasons, any of which will affect the total performance of a film and video.

Meanwhile, the goal of the **theatrical distributor** is to get the film out as soon as possible and to gross as much as possible. This gives him more leverage with the exhibitors for the next picture. Moreover, it means that more marketing dollars need to be spent. (The distributor doesn't care because these dollars are recouped first.) An inflated gross enlarges the distributor's fee and reduces the producer's revenues because the gross is further reduced by marketing recoupment.

At the tail end of the process is the **video company** which wants to see a large P&A commitment and wide-spread theatrical exposure because it benefits directly in terms of units sold. It also wants to release the video as soon as possible after theatrical release, while the film's publicity is still in the public's mind. This makes it difficult for an independent or art film that is distributed territory by territory with just a few prints. It could take six months or a year to play the film on a regional basis. The video manufacturer is accustomed to releasing the video three to six months after the theatrical release. If the film is still playing, a video release could hurt the theatrical box office.

The Deal

The deal's the thing. It's very important to consider the details of a contract carefully, because they can significantly affect your profits.

Setting the Context for Negotiations

The producer's net income depends not only on how well the marketing plan is carried out, but also on how well the deal is negotiated prior to distribution. The film or video distributor always has an advantage over the producer because the distributor supplies the contract and creates the context from which all negotiations spring. If you, as the producer, can turn this around and set your own agenda, you control the direction in which the conversation goes. You start with the standard contract and chip away until it is acceptable. A better strategy is to set the stage by providing the contract (unlikely but possible) for future negotiations; and you therefore may be able to include important issues that normally wouldn't come up.

Basic Contract Terms

The following are basic terms found in most video contracts with comments on how to improve what may be offered. (Theatrical film distribution contracts can be incredibly complex with many more moving pieces, although some of the same elements may appear.)

Exclusive right to distribute. The manufacturer/supplier (e.g., Paramount, Sony, MCA) will want to have the exclusive right to distribute your film on video. Even if they don't distribute to all the markets that the contract covers, they may want to throw a net over other rights in case their distribution expands in the future. Or, they want acquire all the home video rights they can and then go to subdistributors. It is good that the manufacturer try every available venue; but when they subdistribute, rather than doing it themselves, a piece must be paid to the subdistributor and this dilutes the producer's share. If the manufacturer does not sell to special markets, book clubs, or through direct mail, then it is possible for the producer to hold onto these rights.

Besides home video, the producer will have television (pay, basic cable, network, syndication and foreign) as well as book rights, audio rights and merchandising rights. A manufacturer wants as many rights as possible in order to cover the production, acquisition, or marketing costs in the event things do not pan out in home video. Or simply because enough isn't enough.

Advance. An advance is monies advanced to the producer before the video earns royalties. It is royalties received in advance. The producer does not receive any further monies until the program has earned royalties beyond the advance. The advance will be recouped by the distributor (i.e., manufacturer) at the royalty rate.

Note: Many producers do not understand how this works. They assume that if the producer is advanced, say, $50,000, the manufacturer recoups the first $50,000 earned by the video and the producer will receive overages thereafter. This is not how it works.

Of the first $50,000 the producer is entitled to, say, a 20-percent royalty, or $10,000. This $10,000 is recouped by the manufacturer, leaving another $40,000 to be recouped before the producer receives any additional royalties. The program has to earn $250,000 in gross receipts before the $50,000 is recouped at the 20 percent royalty rate.

A manufacturer can also charge interest on money paid out as an advance until it is recouped. In this case, the financing of the production is no different from going to a bank. The producer, not the manufacturer, pays the interest to the bank. Advances should always be non-refundable regardless of how poorly the video performs. The manufacturer takes some risk in putting up an advance because if the video doesn't perform, the manufacturer is out the advance and duplication and marketing costs. If a manufacturer advances money for the production, they may certainly require that an under-budget monies be returned.

Most producers believe that the advance is all the money they will ever see from a production. For a great many this is true, so producers try to get a large fee in the production budget. They may also budget items (office, overhead, equipment rental and the like) that flows back to their own overhead.

Guarantee. A guarantee is like an advance except that payment usually arrives some time in the future. A manufacturer might offer the producer a $100,000 guarantee to be repaid in four payments of $25,000 each every six months beginning six months after the home video release. This allows the video manufacturer to start receiving monies and get some cash flow before paying the producer. Smaller companies that cannot afford large advances use guarantees to acquire programming. Sometimes a producer may receive a larger guarantee than an advance but has to wait for his money. If the producer needs money for production, a guarantee can sometimes be taken to the bank as collateral.

Formats. This refers to all the formats in any and all media, that exist now or may exist in the future. Various formats can include, video cassette (Beta, VHS, 8-mm) and videodisc, and digital, audio, interactive or other formats.

There were no CDs when the Beatles signed their record deal with Capitol. Capitol later interpreted the "any and all media" line to mean that it had the CD rights, but because the CD did not exist at the time the contract was written there was no definition of royalties in the agreements. The Beatles and Capitol haggled over the contract interpretation for some time. It's important to specify that the contract covers only those rights that the parties understand. There are many new format and distribution mechanisms on the horizon, and manufacturers want all format rights in order to protect themselves from unseen technological changes. Remember that various CD, digital and interactive formats are coming into the marketplace. Producers should not be in a great hurry to license these rights without knowing the potential of these media in the markets.

Royalty. Royalties are the monies that the producer receives from the sale and distribution of his video. The definition of royalties is extremely critical. Some manufacturers give and then take away: they agree on a royalty rate in one part of the contract, then, in the boilerplate toward the back of the contract, dilute it with packaging deductions, return allowances, and the like. It is important to use a lawyer familiar with the contract form that the manufacturer is offering. If your lawyer has been in this field of land mines before, you stand a better chance of getting through unscathed.

Original home video programs normally receive a 20-percent royalty. Feature films on home video earn from 25 to 30 percent. In both cases, it's possible to build in escalating royalties that increase at specified sales levels.

Gross Receipts. This term should be interpreted as **all** monies received by the manufacturer from the wholesalers and other accounts, but it usually isn't. The manufacturer's lawyers work long and hard to find as many legitimate deductions as possible to reduce the gross receipts money pool and make royalties significantly smaller. What the producer ends up with is something called "adjusted gross." This is not the same as "gross receipts." Once the producer opens the doors to deductions, he invites more and more dilution. Once he commits to an agreement, any language regarding deductions become legal. What your lawyer negotiates and is reflected in the final contract is the result of how badly the manufacturer wants your program. Your lawyer's job is to push long and hard until he or she comes up to deal-breaking points and must back off.

Returns. Returns can severely batter your royalty. Cassettes are frequently sold on a "guaranteed" or "return" basis. This means that at some future date the wholesaler or rack-jobber can return the cassettes for credit or different product. The manufacturer does not pay a royalty on tapes returned. He didn't make any money on what he thought was a sale, so neither will you. Fair enough. There are two concepts regarding returns *("reserve"* and *"allowance")* which need to be clarified here, so that everyone understands one another and the proper wording appears in the contract.

Returns Reserve. This means that a reserve in the form of a bank account is maintained to cover any returned videos from the wholesalers. The reserve holds money that eventually goes to the producer. The reserve is created because the manufacturer anticipates that video product will be returned and he may have to refund money to some of his buyers. Why is it returned? Because it was sold to the wholesaler (and passed on to the retailer) on the condition that if it didn't sell it could be returned. [Often this is necessary to get buyers to take the product at all.] Since there will be anticipated refunds, the manufacturer does not want to pay all the royalties owed the producer and holds onto some of it in this reserve. The returns reserve is usually from 5 to 20 percent of the royalty and is held until such time as all returns have come back. The time period is negotiable. Some returns come in within six months and others take longer. Because the money in the returns reserve earns interest for the manufacturer or can otherwise be used by him, it is to his benefit to delay its liquidation and ultimate transfer to the producer. Any reserve or money held back from the producer cuts into the royalties until the returns reserve is liquidated. The producer may be able to get the manufacturer to pay him interest on this account. Why not? It's his money the manufacturer is holding.

Returns Allowance. It sounds the same as, and is often talked about as being the same as, a returns reserve, but it has an entirely different meaning. Here one word in the contract can make a significant dent in the producer's bottom line. A *returns* allowance means that the manufacturer is allowed to **deduct and keep** the returns allowance. It is an *allowance*, not a reserve. In such a case the producer can lose as much as the allowance prescribed—maybe as much as 25 percent. His 20-percent royalty can be reduced thereby to a 15 percent royalty.

A producer may think he or she is getting one deal but end up with something very different, since the accounting is based on interpretation of the words and phrases in a contract.

Pricing. Even though prices are stabilizing in the video business, it is difficult to get a manufacturer to commit to one selling price. When the market falls, so do prices, and a manufacturer needs to stay competitive. It serves neither party if the video price is too high in the marketplace.

Contractual language may allow for the reduction of video royalties prorated against the wholesale price. If the wholesale price falls, so does the royalty. (For example, if the retail price starts at $19.95 and falls a year later to $9.95 then the royalty might begin at 20 percent and fall to 10 percent.) Some manufacturers may give different royalties for different classes of trade (rack jobbers, video stores, direct mail, institutional, direct mail, etc.) Different classes of trade get different discounts. It is very difficult to audit and find out what the real selling price may have been. The royalty should be stated specifically in case the selling price is changed. The producer may try to get a fixed dollar amount per cassette rather than a percentage of the gross receipts. While it's tough to negotiate such a deal, you don't have to worry about what price the manufacturer sold the tape at; all you have to know is how many cassettes were manufactered and sold.

215

It makes the math easy. And it makes it tough for accountants to do disappearing acts with your money.

On original or special interest video programs, for example, a producer can get a royalty of 20 percent for a tape with a $29.95 or higher retail price, and 10 percent for anything lower. The 20 percent may look good on paper but the manufacturer can be planning to release the tape at $19.95. Therefore, forget about a 20-percent royalty—you are really getting 10 percent.

Quite frequently a tape is first released at a high retail price for video stores (rentals) and then dropped to a lower price for mass market outlets (sell-through).

Most royalties vary from 10 percent to 20 percent (of gross wholesale receipts), based on the retail price. Therefore, if you can get a commitment from a manufacturer on the pricing, you can tie your royalty (or a dollar amount per tape sold) to the retail price. To cover all contingencies, have the royalties for various retail prices fixed in the contract. That way you always know where you stand.

Release. Specify the release date. Sometimes manufacturers will offer to pay you an acquisition advance for your program **upon release**. This sounds fair, but if the release date changes (or worse yet, never happens) then the producer's advance will come later than anticipated or not at all. The manufacturer could come across a hotter property and bump yours. If the acquisition payment is due when the contract is signed, the manufacturer will bring your video to market sooner to recapture their money. You get your money regardless of the release date. You might negotiate a specific period by which the tape must be released or the rights revert back to you. If the tape isn't released, you won't make any money beyond your advance.

Term. The term is the number of years of the license period with the manufacturer. Since your distribution agreement will be exclusive, the number of years is very important. It could range from a low of a few years to perpetuity. Five or seven or ten years is about average. Sometimes a producer is only able to obtain music clearances for a five-year period, so unless he is able to later extend the music licensing period, he cannot offer the manufacturer a license period beyond five years.

Territories. This refers to the geographic locations in which the manufacturer may sell the program. It could be the U.S., or North America (the U.S. and Canada), or Japan, or it could be worldwide. (If so, the manufacturer will probably use subdistributors in each territory.) You can license your program worldwide yourself by going to manufacturers on a territory-by-territory basis, but, while more lucrative, this is time consuming. You must be able not only to know the business practices of people in other countries but to administer the deals as well. It is also very difficult to supply marketing materials to a variety of manufacturers and coordinate any sort of release. (If it is not coordinated, the opportunity for pirating increases and the pirate can beat the manufacturer to market. This practice has been diminishing in some parts of the world.)

Delivery Date. This is the date specified in the contract by which the producer delivers all the master tapes and "delivery materials" to the manufacturer. The manufacturer needs to fix this date in order to schedule the release date. The producer must understand what these "delivery materials" consist of, in order to not be surprised by additional costs.

Delivery Materials. They include the master videotape, which conforms to specific technical requirements; key artwork; a trailer; errors and omissions insurance (E&O), which protects the manufacturer from rights lawsuits; music and effects (M&E) tracks; a script (or narration transcription); color slides; black-and-white prints; a music cue sheet; and backing rights, agreements and clearances.

If you control the master marketing elements (key artwork and photographs), you have considerable control over the look of the marketing materials. Big stars frequently have approval rights over the photos and art used on the packaging and in publicity.

Holdbacks. A holdback is the period of time during which the program is held back from other media. For example, a feature can be held back from home video distribution for from four to six months. A home video program can be held back from pay cable for six months or more. Or, a pay cable TV program can be held back from home video for some time. Depending on how the program was originally financed, there can be holdbacks in place that must be honored or renegotiated

Marketing Commitment. Although it may be extremely difficult, get a marketing commitment in dollars from your manufacturer. Prior to acquiring or financing a production, he will have assessed the number of cassettes he thinks he can sell. He knows how much to spend to generate that sales level even though he might be unwilling to commit the amount to paper. Without an expenditure of marketing dollars, many promotional, publicity, and marketing strategies will not be employed. The greater expenditure by the manufacturer, the greater his commitment to your program. If he decides to market your video but spends little and it performs poorly, that's the end of the story. If he spends a lot, he'll work much, much harder trying to get his money back. Greater expenditure helps (but does not ensure) wider exposure and makes the program more competitive in the marketplace.

Warranty. Distribution agreements must contain a section in which the rights holder (the producer) represents to the manufacturer that he or she has the right to grant the video rights, including all literary, artistic, musical, and other property rights, to the manufacturer. The producer warrants to the manufacturer that the program is copyrighted.

Indemnity. The producer also indemnifies, or holds harmless, the manufacturer and the manufacturer's licensees, affiliates, employees, and agents against any claims that may occur from other parties.

Accounting Period. The accounting period is the time period after which the producer receives a royalty statement. Manufacturers report quarterly, semi-annually, and annually. Normally the manufacturer sends a royalty report 45 to 60 days after the end of the accounting period (which could be quarterly, semi-annually, or annually).

Audit Rights. Audit rights allow the producer to audit the manufacturer's books during reasonable business hours in case of any dispute over royalties. If a producer thinks that his or her tape is more successful than royalties show, an audit might be in order. Because of the expense of hiring auditors ($10,000 or more), the producer must feel that the royalties reported to date are significantly underreported. Producers whose tapes are hits may want to consider auditing. When there is a lot of money moving through the system, it is prudent to make sure that you are receiving your just desserts. (In this case, find an auditor who has audited your distribution company before. This saves time because he or she will be familiar with the manufacturer's accounting system.)

Use the same strategy when looking for a lawyer to negotiate your distribution contract. Find one who has negotiated contracts with your manufacturer in the past and therefore may be able to start with a pre-negotiated contract. The lawyer might say, *"Listen, we've both got better things to do, so let's just cut through all the bull and start with the same terms that you gave me on that last video deal we did together."* Most likely your lawyer will get something much better than the "standard contract."

Legal fees can run from $50 to $275 per hour. This is not the time to look for bargain-basement lawyers. Your distribution contract is the basis of your entire revenue stream.

Summary

With theatrical films, home video success is often a reflection of how successful the film was when it was original released. For original, special interest programs, success is a result of the pre-promoted elements and the public awareness obtained through marketing and publicity. There are things you can do to increase your video's performance which include having a strong cast, good story, and pre-promoted elements. A most critical moment comes when you sign your distribution contract. Make sure you have legal representation that has dealt with your distributor in the past and knows the ins and outs of the specific distribution agreement.

VIDEO
SPONSORSHIP

VIDEO SPONSORSHIP

"It's like a 'P&A campaign,'except for video. It brings greater consumer awareness and greater sales."

Video Sponsorship

Sponsorship can bring financing. Sponsorship also brings distribution opportunities. It can not be overlooked and is a vital part of producer's financing pallets. There are sponsors, advertisers, and other organizations that supply financing, merchandising, and strategic planning and can make the difference between the success and failure of your project.

Sponsorship

Producers everywhere see sponsorship as a means of financing original video programs, but **most miss the point and pitch sponsors to put up production money.** This is wrong! Not that important! When I say this, producers protest, *"Wiese, are you crazy?"* and I say, *"No."* They miss the point. They aren't thinking of the big picture. Why get only $25,000 or $50,000 toward your production budget when you can get millions in advertising and cross-promotion?

Realize that sponsors have their own agendas. They are trying to sell their services and products, and unless your video can help them do that they won't be interested. If they show interest, suggest cross-promotion (because in your mind you should be thinking how to get your video out in a very big way). Assume you want to produce a series of children's tapes. The sponsor wants to introduce a new product to kids in order to get them to use the product early in their lives and develop a loyalty. Why not have the sponsor commit to promote your video in his next multi-million dollar print and television campaign?

Such a campaign will build far more public awareness about your children's video than the paltry $40,000 most video companies will spend on video marketing for your program. With consumer awareness, you should be able to strike a much better advance deal with a video distributor once the sponsor's promotion ends. And consumers who didn't get the video through the sponsor's promotion can buy it later when it's released through traditional home video distributors.

We've seen numerous examples of sponsorship deals in which a corporation (like Burger King) will use videos (like NINJA TURTLES) for promotional and marketing purposes. Most studios employ product placement services to put together these mega-deals The films are matched to sponsors before and during production.

This marketing model is also being used by video producers to help finance and market their special interest and original programs. The great thing about sponsorship is not that it can bring in production dollars but that it can bring in marketing dollars (both hard and soft) —an often overlooked advantage. **The exposure a video receives because of a sponsor tie-in can amount to a kind of video "P&A campaign," with greater consumer awareness and greater sales.** A sponsor might spend more than $1 million. Of course the sponsor is promoting his own product or service and only incidentally your video, which is merely an adjunct in his campaign. (Remember that sponsors have their own agendas!) Sponsorship supplements other financing. It gives you tremendous leverage in seeking financing from investors or distributors, who readily understand the marketing. So the producer who wants to raise money (or promotion) from a sponsor needs to know something about marketing, too. With a little luck, his payoff can be significant.

Sponsor Deals

Sponsorship deals are as varied as they come. Here are some of the items you can "sell" that will increase your fluency in sponsorship negotiations—you've got to have something to give back in exchange for any form of sponsorship.

A sponsor may use your video in the following ways:

> 1. He has a give-away premium, either a "gift with purchase" or "purchase with purchase."
>
> 2. His product (or service) appears in the video (product placement).
>
> 3. His logo appears on the package and in the titles of the video.
>
> 4. His ad appears at the beginning or end of the video.
>
> 5. He sponsors a resource guide, study guide, booklet, map, poster, or other publication that is included in the video packaging.
>
> 6. All of the above.

A sponsor's primary interest is to reach as many people in his target audience as possible. You can get a sponsor's attention by demonstrating that your video can deliver a new audience for his product. When it comes to proposing the deal, it's better, perhaps, to let the sponsor lead the way. He is adept at putting together promotion ideas. The producer's role is to act as a catalyst and be fast on his or her feet when it comes to putting the deal together. You may, of course, suggest ideas, but it is the sponsor who best knows his own needs.

The demographics of the typical video renter is divided equally between male and female. He/she is 37 years old and has an income of $41,000 and some college education. His/her household has 3.5 people (2.2 adults, 0.44 teens and 0.74 pre-teens). The video renter goes to the video store 56 times a year and spend 20 hours a year there.

Video producers have had a difficult time speaking the same language as the ad agencies and corporate developments that buy video sponsorship. The advertisers and sponsor think in terms of "impressions"—lots of them, and the real obstacle in determining the worth of a home video rental tape to advertisers is measuring these impressions. The cost per thousand (of impressions) needs to be very low compared to that of television since the sponsors think in terms of television audience buys.

A **rental tape** has more impressions in its life than a **sell-through tape** that remains in a consumer's home. The value of the impression to someone who went to the effort to rent or buy a video is considerably greater than it is to someone just sitting in front of network television. The selection process is far greater than simply turning on the tube— video is a very "focused medium" because consumers pay to watch tapes. Advertisers feel the home video viewer has greater motivation to take action and buy their products than the average television viewer has.

While movies and other highly visible entertainment forms are the best vehicles for video advertising, that does not rule out video how-to's and some event programs. The Fairfield Group, a video marketing researcher, interviewed consumers to find out the most acceptable genres for video sponsorship, with the following result:

Genre	Percent Acceptable
Action/adventure	21%
Drama	15%
Kidvid	13%
Sports	8%
Comedy	7%

This may give you an idea of how suitable your genre is for video sponsorship.

How to Figure Impressions

There is no generally accepted formula that guarantees the number of impressions a sponsor's ad makes on its video audience. Because sponsors are used to thinking in terms of impressions, you must come up with logical scenarios they can understand. Since advertisers like to talk in thousand of impressions, video producers have come up with various formulas for figuring impressions to help convince potential sponsors about the reach of a video program.

Here's one formula that can be presented to sponsors. Since sponsors may be accustomed to spending far less per thousand than this model, you need to make the argument that your video deserves a better price because it delivers a highly-targeted self-selecting audience.

An **"A" feature film** (defined as grossing more than $30 million at the box office) will sell at least 300,000 copies (at $89 retail). It may sell millions of copies at a $24.95 sell-through—see below for definition of this term—price, but then you won't have as large a number of impressions per tape). Multiply this by the number of rentals in each tape's lifetime, say 100, and multiply again by the number of people who will see the tape at each viewing, say 2.5. Using these

227

assumptions, you have an "A" title video that will yield 75 million impressions.

What is the value of 75 million impressions? Let's assume further that an advertiser might pay $25 per thousand highly-targeted names (mailing lists cost $50 per thousand names). As 75 million is 75 thousands multiply that by $25 to get a value of $1,875,000 for "A" title video impressions.. On the basis of these numbers you could ask an advertiser for $1,875,000 (in cash or advertising barter, or both) to put his ad or message at the head of this hot "A" title. This assumes that your title and his target audience match precisely, as the advertiser will not want to put his ad on a video he perceives as too sexy or violent, or contrary to the image he wishes to perpetuate.

Let's drop down to a **"B" title** retail and assume it will sell 50,000 units at $69 retail. Since it is a "B," it will rent only 30 times in its lifetime. Keeping all other assumptions the same ($25 per thousand value x 2.5 viewers), its value is $93,750.

Now let's examine *"sell-through product,"* tapes that sell to one consumer and may be viewed by two people. Unlike rental product, these tapes do not have large numbers of people viewing them because they are owned and not lent. An exercise tape selling 100,000 units will generate 250,000 impressions and have a value of $6,250. Even so, you might go to four non-competing sponsors (say a shoe company, a sweat shirt manufacturer, a soft drink manufacturer, and a vitamin company), and offer to promote each product within the tape, and in addition give them ads and on-package advertising. If successful, that strategy could yield $25,000 ($6,250 each) toward your budget or in advertising and promotion from the sponsors. While $25,000 might not seem like much, every little bit helps, and the promotion that the four sponsors could lend to the video can be significant. It certainly gives your tape visibility that it wouldn't get in any other way.

As with art, it is the sponsor who places a value on your video, so this particular impression value calculation may not be as useful as it seems. Basically, *"it's what you can get for it."*

TOP GUN, PLATOON, DIRTY DANCING, and TEENAGE MUTANT NINJA TURTLES all had national corporate sponsors participating in marketing and cross-promotions campaigns.

Premiums

Premiums are a $10 billion-a-year business. Premiums can be almost anything that is given away free (or used as a "purchase with purchase") to promote sales of other products and services—usually an unimaginative stream of pens, T-shirts, coffee mugs, note pads, clocks, paperweights, and thousands of other items, sometimes imprinted with the company or product name. A whole industry is devoted to selling premiums to corporations, charities, and other sponsors. A leading magazine in this market is <u>Premium and Incentive</u>. Because video has a high perceived value among consumers but a low price to corporate buyers, it has arrived as a coveted premium.

Like their cousins—the personalized coffee mug and baseball hat —videos have entered the premium market. Why? Consumers know videos cost $19.95, $39.95, $89.95, or more. If they can get one free with a purchase, or as a low-cost purchase-with-a-purchase, they feel it's a great deal, and they feel great about the sponsor. Many advertisers and their clients use videos to draw in new consumers for their products because video delivers a very targeted demographic. Burger King's video promotion using TEENAGE MUTANT NINJA TURTLES sold well over 10 million units. With new videos coming out every few weeks, kids and their families develop a Burger King Whopper habit, which is the real goal of this premium (or incentive) program.

These big premium deals are few and far between for most producers.

There are, however, many companies that might buy 5,000, or 10,000, or even 100,000 videos if they felt it expanded the market for their core product. A premium deal in the bag can help finance your program. How does this work? Say you are making a one-hour how-to program. You make a deal with a company that you will cut a "special version" (half hour) of the program for them, with special packaging and their promotional spot on the tape. They pay you $1 each (it could be a tad more or less) over actual manufacturing costs for 50,000 units. That's $50,000 you can put into the production. They have a premium tape, you have some financing, and you own the rights to a longer version of the program for the video markets. Everyone wins.

Who Are Prospective Sponsors?

The primary question is, *Who are the buyers and what do they want?* Without an answer to that, you cannot even begin.

Video marketers are always looking for new ways to merchandise video, and for new opportunities to cross-promote a video with other products, thereby maximizing promotional and advertising dollars. A sponsor may put an ad on the video to promote a product or service and, in exchange, give the video distributor an additional marketing push through the sponsor's ongoing consumer advertising programs. There will be some promotional tie-in between the sponsor's product and the video (e.g., the partnerships between TOP GUN and Pepsi, DIRTY DANCING and Nestle).

Video retailers want the distributors to advertise on radio and, especially, television, and in newspapers and magazines when the videos are released, so that people will be driven into the video stores to rent or purchase cassettes. No doubt the video trade magazines will tout the relationship between an upcoming title and a sponsor willing to spend large dollars for consumer advertising. This encourages the video retailer to anticipate larger-than normal-requests for rental and he therefore may buy-in more copies.

Manufacturer's Point of View

Eavesdropping at a Billboard/AFI-sponsored American Video Conference, I found it clear that manufacturers/suppliers are exceptionally interested in video sponsorship. However, rather than have their marketing staff take on this task, they prefer that the producer deliver a sponsor along with the program ideas. It's not that the suppliers are unwilling to finance productions, it's that they want the reassurance that there will be more marketing clout behind the program when its release date arrives. **The job of soliciting and landing sponsors is falling more and more into the lap of the producer.**

The best way to approach sponsors is to show that you have something to offer them—**from their point of view**—that just can't be passed up. That means you must have some understanding of their needs (and not just your own) to get financing and marketing support. Your program must inspire and motivate their target audience without leaving any negative impression that could soil their corporate image.

Note: The search for PBS underwriting is not too different from the search for video sponsorship. Both seek to deliver programming (and audiences) to corporations, who in turn are looking to promote their goods, services, and good name.

As you develop an idea for a program, think about sponsors who would be the most likely partners. Once you've identified the candidates, study what they do and how they do it before approaching them. When you meet, make it very clear what benefits (to them) can be derived from sponsoring your project.

231

Getting money may be your need, but producing is certainly not theirs. Besides their value to you may lie beyond production dollars. Think marketing. **A link with your potential sponsor's marketing, promotion, and distribution resources could give your video a tremendous push.** You must study what resources they have at hand before you suggest such a deal. You must also be fast on your feet because they may very likely offer promotional uses and tie-ins that you hadn't thought of, and you will need to see whether these ideas will benefit your program as well.

One way to determine the feasibility of a tie-in is to find sponsors who do a good job promoting their own products or services. Do they use premiums, giveaways, proof-of-purchase offers, or coupons? If so, your tape may make a good premium. It will be easy to pitch because they already understand premiums and their value in selling their own products.

Remember though, that **sponsors have a different agenda than you have**. They are not interested in selling your video. They want to sell their service or product and **your video must help them accomplish this task**. This is the point at which the thinking of most producers falls short.

Don't sell your program only on what a great idea it is, but also on how well it ties in with your sponsor's product. Audience demographics and the penetration your tape can make into new markets for their product or service are most important to them. Let them know all the ways the tape will be distributed; if you don't, they may think that they are doing all the work to get distribution for your program. (And that may be true.) Come in with a national video distributor who can provide a marketing plan. That gives you more clout. Don't come with your hand out—you have to bring something to the party.

Get multiple, non-competing sponsors for your tape if you can. An exercise tape could have a shoe manufacturer, a soft drink company, a sportswear manufacturer and a vitamin company as sponsors. If they all cross-promoted and marketed your tape through their own outreach, public awareness could be significantly greater than you'd normally get through traditional distribution channels. What if you tied in a large national magazine as well? Maximize resources. Create synergy by combining powerful third and fourth parties where everybody wins.

What is Sponsorable?

What is your tape about? Who is the primary audience? What is their income? Where do they live? What are their interests? If you were to follow them around for a week of shopping, what would they buy? The manufacturers of the products in the audience's shopping bags may make up a hit list for sponsorship! This is, of course, an oversimplification, but it gives you the idea. You want to get inside the lifestyle of the consumer as much as possible to see which products and services they use and if a video-to-sponsor match is possible.

If you decide to produce a video for teenage girls and you don't know much about their buying and living habits, buy an armload of teen magazines for an overview of potential sponsors who sell cosmetics, food, clothes, and records to teenage girls. A whole universe will open up. Depending on your program, the buyer may <u>not</u> be the teen but the mother or grandmother who purchases the program for her daughter or granddaughter. This may mean that your sponsor has to reach the mother or grandmother in order to reach the teen.

Big sponsorship deals happen with "A" movie titles. Disney did a promotion with MacDonald's and released a LADY AND THE TRAMP promotion into 65,000 fast-food restaurants. This, combined with Disney's superb marketing, sold over 3 million videos. Both Disney and MacDonald's speak to families: Disney for entertainment, MacDonald's for food. It was a great match.

A more unlikely but also successful match was Nestle and DIRTY DANCING. (See the market case study in Wiese's book, Film & Video Marketing.) The video sold 375,000 units. Nestle's promotion kicked in after the video release, which extended the normal selling period for a video. The tape returned to the number one spot on the charts six weeks after its release, which is very unusual. Nestle got a commercial on the videotape and their logo on the cassette package and promotional materials. Vestron's (the producing firm's) tape was promoted in magazine and TV ads paid by Nestle. The movie's demographics are very broad and so are Nestle's. They used this opportunity to promote white chocolate to a new audience through a new medium.

Crystal Light sponsored a Championship Aerobic Workout that Lorimar released as a video. The tape gained additional credibility by being tied in with a national aerobics organization. Not only did the organization lend a stamp of approval to the exercise method, but it gave the sponsors visibility before their national membership. The tape had an exclusive "first window" of sales through Crystal Light, a beverage. Initially, the only way a consumer could get the video was if he also bought Crystal Light. Crystal Light and the tape were distributed by General Foods, which did free-standing inserts (F.S.I.) in 46 million newspapers. Not bad for a humble original program. That exposure gave the tape a presence because—once the premium window expired and the tape was released through the normal video outlets—people recognized the video from Crystal Light's promotion and that may have made them more likely to buy or rent it.

An advertiser can help a tape get tremendous exposure that is way beyond the resources of a video distributor. Distributor support in the marketing of a tape is far more important in the long run than having the distributor pay for its production. Distributors don't care about the production—they care about the tape's outreach. And so should the producer and the video manufacturer.

One of the first and most successful video sponsorships was the TOP GUN/Pepsi promotion. A special TV commercial featuring Pepsi that looked like a scene out of the movie (but wasn't) was shown with a tag that let people know the video was available for $24.95 instead of $29.95. This ad made it look as if the price were low because Pepsi helped defray costs. (Not really true.) The good guys at Pepsi were perceived—thanks to their own ads—as giving the consumer a break on the video. Pepsi spent several million dollars on the TV spots and print ads. Over 2.5 million videotapes were sold.

The Exchange

When you find a prospective sponsor there are no rules. It's time to be imaginative because more likely than not you'll be making up the deal as you go along. If a sponsor shows interest he already has a promotion idea in mind and it connects in some way with their marketing plans. What can you offer a sponsor?

Here is a checklist of ideas and sponsor benefits:

> 1. An association with an image, idea, message, or form of entertainment that is a positive link between the sponsor and a targeted viewing audience.

> 2. A new means to distribute the sponsor corporate message or product in a new environment (video) to a new (or existing) audience.

> 3. The ability to associate the sponsor corporate image with _____ (fill in the blank). (It could be a star, a football team, a big movie, or an innovative program.)

> 4. A promotional spot at the head or tail of the tape.

5. The sponsor's corporate logo on the packaging.

6. A sponsor presentation title. *"Pepsi Presents..."*

7. An opportunity to put sponsor coupons inside the video cassette packaging. *("Get 10 percent off on our product with this coupon." "Try our new product and we'll rebate $1 to you.")*

8. A vehicle to demonstrate the sponsor product (e.g., a how-to bicycle tape featuring the manufacturer's bicycles). The sponsor's product or service may be a subtle or not so subtle element in the program.

In exchange your sponsor may provide:

1. Production funds.

2. Goods or services during production (food, clothing, props, cars...)

3. Magazine or newspaper advertising featuring the video.

4. A special promotion for the video.

5. A national tour for the tape's host, celebrity, or spokesperson.

6. The advertiser's national spokesperson for an appearance in the video.

7. A well-known trademark that can bring credibility and additional perceived value to the program.

8. Many other innovative and valuable resources that you will not even think of until you begin your brainstorming sessions with the sponsor.

Keep in mind that the sponsor's primary use of a video program is as an advertising medium and perhaps a promotional premium.

It may take some research to find the right person to pitch this to. Corporations are large and it can be difficult to determine who has the authority to make the decision you want. You may have to shuttle between an advertising agency and the sponsor's product manager, or you may have to work through the promotion or corporate communications (public relations) department. At some point you may have to pitch the sales and marketing group. Always address each group with a presentation on the benefits to be derived through their association and participation in your project.

Finding a sponsor can take an unbelievable amount of time, a year or more. Big deals are not a result of quick pitches where everyone says, *"Yes, let's do it,"* and you're off and running. There are committees and corporate strategy and budgetary periods. Corporate officers are very cautious—no one wants to make a mistake—so decisions are frequently made and remade and second-guessed. Megalithic corporations plan strategies **years in advance**. By the time you talk to them, they are already a year or two down the road in implementing what they will do. On the other hand, you can sometimes be in the right place at the right time and things can happen very fast.

Vestron's sponsorship deal with Nestle came through serendipity. Nestle already had a promotion lined up with another product but it fell through. Vestron was there with DIRTY DANCING as a replacement in the final hour. Previously, many other sponsors turned down what turned out to be one of the largest-grossing independent films with a record-breaking soundtrack album.

Video is a highly competitive business. Sponsorship brings significant clout to the marketing effort and increases a program's chance for visibility and for success. A sponsored video deal would be very interesting to just about any video supplier or manufacturer (e.g., Paramount, J2, Media, etc.) Sponsorship gives the video marketer considerably more resources to work with. It is very difficult, however, to get a sponsor **without** a video manufacturer in place. The sponsor wants to know that the video will get widespread distribution. Sometimes producers have to be creative and juggle deals with both video manufacturers and sponsors simultaneously until a ménage à trois can be arranged.

National Organizations

A national organization carries its own kind of endorsement. The right name enhances the awareness and perceived value of a tape. Would you rather buy a first-aid tape with the logo of the Red Cross or the Detroit General Hospital on it? A stop-smoking tape without an endorsement from Smoke-Enders would be a missed opportunity. Magazines also bring their own audiences. In some cases it makes sense to co-produce with a magazine and use its imprimatur. A magazine sponsor may be useful in providing advertising space and coupons, and helping with other cross-promotions.

THE ASTRONOMERS: Sponsorship and Marketing Promotion

The major PBS series, THE ASTRONOMERS, received more than $5 million from the Keck Foundation for production. Keck also contributed to the advertising for the series, and got presenter's credit on the broadcast, in the home video version, and in all publicity and newspaper ads. A large new telescope that Keck built in Hawaii also received brief coverage within one of the programs.

Once the series was finished, I worked for PBS Home Video designing marketing elements for the six-volume video collection. Marketing isn't the same as financing, but it's included here because every dollar that you save during the whole process from production through distribution is a dollar that you don't have to raise. Cross-promotion is a close cousin of sponsorship, and like sponsorship can dramatically increase the sales of your video without dramatically increasing your costs. If you can figure out any marketing that will increase the income potential of your program(s), this is an additional incentive to potential investors and distributors.

Here's a sketch of some of the things that were done on THE ASTRONOMERS:

Initial printing was 25,000 six-volume sets. The programs sell for $19.95 each or $129.95 for the whole set. (Anybody able to multiply will see that it costs $10.25 more if you buy the set than if you buy the volumes individually. Then what's the motivation to buy the set? Other elements and goodies were added to increase the perceived value of the set (that did not cost the manufacturer very much more for the extra income of $10, or $250,000, from the first printing). Here's what "extras" consumers got when they bought the set:

- A free book, <u>Your Personal Guide to the Night Sky</u>.
- A coupon for a discount on the consumer's own telescope.
- A coupon for a discount membership in the Astronomical Society.
- A coupon for a discount on <u>Omni</u> magazine.
- A coupon for a FREE music video utilizing special effects from the series.
- A coupon for the book, <u>The Astronomers</u>.

The total package was substantial but these merchandising add-ons cost little or nothing. For example, an agreement with the telescope

239

company and the Astronomical Society promised outreach to a very targeted audience, many of whom would be very interested in a telescope or membership in the Society. Coupons in 25,000 sets (times 6 videos) reached 150,000 people. Not only did the coupons give the consumer a bonus, but they were enormously valuable to both the telescope people and the Astronomical Society, and this enabled THE ASTRONOMERS videos to get the following in trade:

• A free ad in 200,000 catalogs that go to 45,000 Astronomical Society members, schools and institutions.

• Re-publication of the Society's book into a smaller format for free inclusion in the set. (A small licensing fee was paid.)

• An agreement that the telescope company would put a flyer about THE ASTRONOMERS video collection in 150,000 telescope boxes over the next two years.

Side deals are also made for the purchase of telescopes (at a very low premium price). These telescopes were given away free to video retailers who purchased an ASTRONOMERS floor display (which holds 24 titles or 4 sets). The telescopes were enormously popular and helped drive sales. Retailers used them in floor displays, gave them away as prizes to their customers or sales people, or kept the telescopes for themselves.

A great many other cross promotions took place. For example, the free ASTRONOMERS music video was not only given away to consumers but used by the press department for publicity purposes and to attract greater attention for the series. On TV talk shows, the astronomers who appeared in the programs talked over the music video images. This gave the talk show guests much more to present. News programs were able roll the great images under their end credits. The music video was also was used by the sales department to motivate their young telemarketers. *"Hit your goal and get a very cool music video."*

St. Martins Press published THE ASTRONOMERS book. There was a straight promotion trade: the book contained a "blow-in" coupon promoting the tape collection and the video promoted the book through an enclosed coupon.

There were many other cross promotion deals that took place. What happens is that everyone wins. Everyone gets more spin on his own product by working in tandem with others to reach common markets. More promotion brings greater consumer awareness to all the products. The key is finding products (and services) that appeal to the audience each marketer is trying to reach.

SPORTS MANUFACTURER AS FINANCIER

A sponsored deal can also be beneficial in getting a program produced. Here's an example in which a sports equipment manufacturer was the key element in financing a specialty video program. This scenario may give you fresh ideas about other manufacturers to pursue:

The manufacturer of a certain sporting good wanted a consumer tape (a subtle long-form commercial or infomercial) that featured his product. He owned and operated several retail stores where a tape could be sold. (The manufacturer assumed he could use the video for in-store and sales purposes—so he'd get more bang for his buck.) A little research revealed that very few tapes, if any, had been produced on the specialized sports activity that used the manufacturer's product.

A director with expertise in the sport brought the manufacturer and the owner of a video production facility to the table to make a deal between them. The manufacturer agreed to buy 10,000 units (at a wholesale price of $10 each) from the director/production facility. The $100,000 would be paid in advance and used for the production. (The budget was $75,000.) All other rights in the program would remain with the director and the production facility, which meant the director could also sell the videotape through traditional video distribution.

The sports manufacturer (the sponsor) had tapes to sell (and could make a profit on those tapes) that would help defer his investment. He also got a tape featuring his product for sales and promotional purpose and was delighted to learn that the video could also be distributed elsewhere, because his product was prominently featured! (And he didn't request or demand any royalty participation in the video even though he had financed it.)

The producer/production facility could put the $25,000 that the manufacturer paid into their pockets or they could use it for marketing in a self-distribution scenario. Or they might take it to a video distributor and cut a better than average deal because they could put up the $25,000 for marketing costs.

Without the participation of the manufacturer, the video (given its subject matter) would be a difficult program to finance. Small deals like this are just waiting to happen. You must be inventive about how a tape can benefit consumers and sponsors. Producers must educate manufacturers on how they benefit from sponsoring video. They must also educate themselves so that the deals they offer the manufacturers really do make sense, which means understanding marketing and what the sponsor would benefit from. It's not enough to want to make a video. The sponsor must see an advantage before he will plunk down dollars.

A producer who can think all the way through the production process to the point where his program is finished—and then asks himself how can it be best marketed—may come up with all kinds of innovative things he can do at the beginning of his project that will bring money, cross-promotions, and marketing into the production. The more elements that can be put into place, the more powerful the package, and the more attractive it will be to investors and the variety of

242

distributors in different media that the producer will be utilizing. The great thing about cross-marketing is that it is either low cost or free. Repeat this three times: *Money you don't have to spend is money you don't have to raise.*

Agents for Sponsorship

As home video as a promotional device becomes more understood by sponsors and advertisers, they will find new uses for it. Producers, too, must find new ways to present their ideas to advertisers and corporations when designing videos. It is difficult to know exactly where to begin and what kind of deal to suggest. Looking across the table at one another can be pretty strange for both producers and advertisers, especially if they aren't able to speak the same language. But as the benefits of video sponsorship become apparent, a mutual desire to work together will grow.

To help bridge the gap between sponsors and distributors, a new kind of agent or consultant, who serves as a marriage counselor between advertisers and sponsors, has sprung up. Sometimes he is aware of sponsors looking to enter home video who need fresh concepts. The marriage counselor consults with producers, helping them shape and position their programs appropriately for sponsorship. He may make the presentation, either alone or with the producer. Some major ad agencies have departments devoted to movie and video sponsorship. There are also product placement companies, mostly in Los Angeles and New York, that develop home video sponsorship deals. To find the most active agents, when you see a sponsored video promotion, call the marketing departments of the studios, ad agencies, or corporations and ask who put the deal together. Then call them.

Video sponsorship is still new. Corporations and advertisers alike are becoming more sophisticated in how to use it. Producers who have the time to spend and who understand corporate and advertising needs may be able to put together some very large sponsorship deals.

243

After all, an order for 10,000 to 100,000 or 1,000,000 videos can get you into production very quickly. With an order this large, you don't have to find a distributor. The sponsor is the distributor.

SO MANY QUESTIONS, SO LITTLE TIME

SO MANY QUESTIONS, SO LITTLE TIME

"Getting it done is asking yourself the right questions."

The Clearing Process

You've read the book. You've absorbed a lot of information. Some of it will be useful and some of it won't, depending on the kind of project you are putting together and the resources you have. Think of the ideas in the book as colors on your palette that you can use in a variety of ways to accomplish your goals.

Now it's time to go into action. Write down answers to the following questions, which address very specific issues. Questions that remain unanswered mean you still have preparatory work to do.

The whole process of producing is finding the answers to the right questions through meeting people and asking for and getting support. Producing consists of a series of many small steps, and if you line them up beforehand you can save a lot of time—years perhaps. That's why it's important to find out what you need by asking yourself these questions.

Questions for Financial Success

Financial success? Well, maybe. Maybe not. But if you set your mind on being successful you'll find yourself a lot more capable of accomplishing your task than if you tell yourself how difficult it all is.

Ask yourself these questions one at a time. It helps to break the steps down and gives your mind smaller tasks to work on, which feel possible.

247

Let your mind be creative. Toss up any and all ideas. Perhaps you can use a tape recorder, then transcribe your ideas later. (This prevents the act of writing from getting in the way.) First time around you are in the information hunting and gathering stage, so don't be critical of the answers you get.

Go through this process more than once, and give yourself plenty of time to answer each question. By putting them into your subconscious mind, you will be working on the questions constantly. You may get answers at strange times, so have a scratch pad nearby to write them down. Sometimes you may not get a specific answer but will have a subtle feeling about what to do. Pay attention and give yourself a chance to interpret it. This can be helpful in reaching your goal.

Once you've received answers to all your questions, evaluate them. In some cases your ego gives answers that will hinder rather than help your project. This is not unusual because, after all you thought up the idea for the film or video, and your ego may be unwilling to find fault with it. If you find yourself skimming over or taking these questions lightly (*"Oh, I know that. Oh, that one's not important."*), your ego may be in the driver's seat.

From consulting with hundreds of producers, it is my experience they find it difficult to be honest about the real market place value of their project. Producers frequently fantasize about the wealth their project will create. That's what keeps them going, but at the same time, we need to make sure what we tell ourselves is possible. Honesty to one's self and to one's partners, investors, and others is critically important.

Here are the questions:

The Project
- What do I want to make?
- Why?
- What do I hope to realize in terms of financial return?
- Why?
- Do I have the stuff to stick with **this project** for the next two years? Five years?
- Do I have the ability, resources, and contacts to produce this project myself?

Partners
- What kind of person is an ideal partner?
- What kind of skills should he or she have?
- With whom could I partner?
- What would attract him or her to this project?

Packaging & Presentation
- Who are agents that represent projects like this?
- Who are producers and others who can assist me?
- Who can help me prepare a presentation? Graphics? Layout?
- Who can write it?
- Who can prepare financial statements and income projections?
- Have I rehearsed my presentation well in front of friends before presenting it to investors?
- Can I capture the interest of investors with my presentation?
- What's the strongest part? The weakest? How do I know that? Is anything missing?
- Do I have "letters of intent" from co-creators, writers, actors, distributors?
- Do I have these documents: completion bond, insurance policy, partnership papers, agreements with talent and creative partners?
- Is my project fully packaged (script, talent, production facility, director, producer, writer, budget, schedule, commitment letters)?
- What promotable elements are part of my package?

249

• Have I consulted with marketing and publicity experts to predetermine the hooks and promotable elements in my film or video? What are the hooks? Which hooks can be amplified? What new hooks or elements are needed?

Budget and Rights
• What will it cost?
• Has my budget been professionally prepared?
• Am I certain it is accurate?
• Have I made assumptions about deferrals or special deals that could fall through? Did I delete them from my budget?
• Have I cleared all the rights in the project (story, book, music, talent, etc.)?
• Do I know the exact cost of these rights?

The Market
• Is there a market for my film or video?
• How do I know that?
• What does my project offer that attracts a distributor?
• What does my project have that interests an audience?
• What does my project have that appeals to the media and generates publicity?
• Will people want to see my film or video more than once? Why?
• What are the elements (actors, story, marketing, etc.) that will make it successful?

Income Projections
• What returns can I expect?
• What other films or videos have had similar performances?
• Have I researched the market for this specific project?
• Do I know the film or video potential in each market?
• Do I know how revenues flow back to me from rights sales and licenses?
• Do I know the deductions and fees subtracted by distributors and agents before the money reaches me?

• Is there a significant upside or do expected revenues cover the budget and no more?

Development
• Am I good at developing properties? If not, how can I find them?
• Have I skills for developing profitable, worthwhile projects, or am I better at getting it produced once it's selected? Is there someone I can partner with who's good at development if that's not my strong point?
• Do I have the time and resources to develop a property?
• Should I try to raise development money?
• Do I know how risky this is?
• Do I know how to structure a development deal with investors?
• Am I able to incorporate promotable elements within my story or video idea?
• What are they?
• Can I call upon contacts within large and small literary agencies for scripts to read?
• Do I know how a development deal works with a studio?

Resources
• Do I know how and where to commission key art and/or package art for my project?
• What skills do I need in my support team?
• Am I or do I have a charismatic salesperson with highly developed communication skills who can pitch the project?
• Have I a lawyer in place who can turn "letters of interest" into formal agreements?
• Have I an accountant to prepare the financial structures that are necessary?
• Have I a production company with a track record to handle the physical production of the film or video?
• Have I letters of intent from the principal participants that can be converted to contracts?
• Have I a financial vehicle through which to raise financing?

251

• Do I have a professionally prepared budget that accurately reflects both above-the-line and below-the-line costs?
• Have I examined each and every line item to find potential savings?
• Do I need a completion bond company? Why? Do I have a completion bond company in place?
• Have I identified the banks that finance film and video production?
• Have I contacted the guilds and unions? Have I been able to make any special deals?
• Have I found a lab or post-production facility that will cut a deal?
• Am I willing to negotiate for everything? If not, do I have someone that is?
• Have I explored deferred payments with everyone involved with the production?
• Have I found an advertising company that might exchange ad time for equity?
• Have I identified the best distributors for my project?
• Have I decided whether to approach them with my package or will I wait until my film is finished? Why?
• Do I have an agent who can get me into the studios?
• Do I know what impresses a banker? Can I make a presentation to a banker in his own terms and leave my normal exhilarated pitch at home?
• Do I understand there are very few people whose names alone are bankable?

Income Projections
• Are my income projections based on similar projects? Really?
• Am I able to put my desires aside and objectively assess the financial upside of my project?
• Has my project been financially researched by someone experienced with each market and with how cash flows (after deductions) to the producer?

Deferrals

• Who will defer some or all of their salaries?
• What are the facilities that exchange services for equity in the project?
• Where do people stand in relation to one another in the flow of revenues?
• Who comes first? Who comes last? Who shares at the same level (equity partners, producers, deferrals, investors, interest, bank, loans, etc.?)

Investors

• Who is willing to invest in my project?
• Who—among my friends or family—will loan or invest money in it?
• Who do I know that will introduce me to an investor or lender in my project?
• Do my lawyer, family, co-producer, or others know potential investors?
• Who has supported my work in the past?
• What former employers will help in my financing search?
• Do I know a banker that will loan money?
• Can I borrow against my equity in a house or property?
• Are there companies within or without the film/video business interested in participating in some manner in this project?
• Are there corporate sponsors I can approach?
• Are there manufacturers, airlines, or service companies that may donate or invest by providing the production with equipment, airline tickets, hotels, food, clothes, cars, etc.?
• Do I know a lawyer who will work for equity in the project?
•Are there any blocks between me and raising money? What? What do I need to do to make those blocks go away? Am I willing to do it?

Pre-Sale Agents
• What distributors have handled similar films or videos?
• Who are they? In the U.S.? In Europe? In Asia?
• Will they pre-buy rights?
• Historically, what income have they generated, what advances or pre-buy payments and deals have they made?
• What producers did they make these deals with? (Have I found and talked with them? What was their advice?)
• Is my attorney watching over the project and all negotiations?
• Do I need to make pre-sales in order to fully or partially finance my project?
• Do I know the value of a pre-sale for my particular genre?
• Have I found a reputable foreign sales agent?
• Is he someone I feel good about working with?
• Does he attend all the major film and video markets?
• What kind of sales record has he had for his other producers?
• Am I confident my sales agent knows the major foreign buyers, and isn't simply sub-licensing through other agents?
• Do I have a trailer, key art, or other materials my sales agent can use?
• Have I explored domestic pay television for financing? Satellite companies? Pay-per-view?
• Have I actors with name value in foreign markets?

Risk Capital
• Am I offering a fair deal to my investors?
• Is it competitive with alternative investments they could make?
• Am I aware that different pitches attract different investors, depending on their perception of the world?
• Am I aware of how important my own integrity, enthusiasm, and ability to create a vision are in obtaining investments?

• Do I know what it means to obtain *critical mass* in my package? What's missing? What will enable me to do so?

• Are my investors also *end-users* who can help get distribution?

• Do I know what investors want?

• Am I aware that investors run to *abundance* and run from *scarcity*?

• Do I have more investors lined up than I need? Why not?

• Can I get the names of two potential investors for every "no" I receive?

• Has my lawyer explained state laws and SEC regulations about raising money to me?

• Do I understand how limited partnerships work? Have I structured my deal in a competitive and equitable fashion?

• Do I understand how letters of credit work?

• Is it desirable to have someone else raise the money for me? Why? Why not?

• Have I prepared a "hit list" of potential investors?

• Am I willing to network with virtually everyone I come into contact with?

• What am I doing to get visibility for my project?

• Are there television, home video, corporations, or other buyers that might want an equity position in my project?

• Have I found a foreign sales agent?

• How many markets do I wish to pre-sell to finance my production?

• What markets will give me an upside?

• Have I identified co-production partners?

• Can I use below-the-line deals in foreign countries?

• Can I raise P&A and rent-a-distributor money?

Pre-sales

• What is my pre-sale strategy?

• What is the real opportunity for pre-selling rights in my film?

• Is it a pre-sale genre? What percent of my budget can I really expect to raise?
• Have I found a reputable pre-sale agent? How long has he been in business?
• Have I pre-sold domestic pay television?
• Are my actors known internationally?
• Am I assured of a U.S. release? Do I have a U. S. distributor in place?
• Do I understand how cash flows back to me from the sales agent?
• Do I understand how revenues from distribution come back to me? Deductions?
• Do I understand how to save money by producing with local currency in foreign countries?
• Am I lining up financing and distribution at the same time? Why? Why not?

Distribution
• Is my best strategy to engage the financing and support of a distributor before production or when the film is finished? Why?
• Is it realistic to think a major studio will make a "negative pickup deal" for this project? Who might? Why?
• Is it realistic to think an independent distributor will "pick up" my film? Who might? Why?
• Is it realistic to think a studio video distributor will acquire my video? Who? Why? What reasons?
• Is it realistic to think an independent video distributor will acquire my video?
• Is there a foreign market for my film or video? Do I have a star with foreign appeal? What else?
• What is the greatest advance I can expect to get from a studio or independent specialty distributor? Why do I think that? What have these companies recently paid for other similar-genre films?
• Who will negotiate my deal with a distributor, financiers, and/or

investors? A lawyer, a producer's rep, or me? Are they experienced?
• Who will negotiate special deals like sponsorship, facilities deals, deferments? Are they experienced?
• Are my negotiation skills strong enough?
• Am I, or is someone else, able to conceive all the financial elements necessary to put my project together? Can all the pieces be tailored to fit financially and legally and can I still offer my investors (if any) an attractive return? (Am I able to clearly map out this strategy?)
• Have I found investors, actors, facilities, distributors and others—all of whom have a real stake in my project—who can continue to promote the film to insure profits once the film is completed?
• Am I aware of the degree that domestic distribution will bring value to my film in the foreign markets?
• Are my deals with my distributors equitable? Is everyone appropriately awarded for the risks they have taken or will take?

Financing
• Have I taken the time to design a strategy, game plan, and "hit list" for my financing efforts?
• What do I think the best route or combination of routes is? Why?
• Are my partners strong and do they really bring something to the party?
• Are my attorney and accountants experienced with the film and/or video business?
• Is my investor deal appealing? Does it communicate that I'm looking out for my investors' interest?
• Have I thought about the advantages and disadvantages of pre-selling my rights?

Resources
• Do I get a good feeling from the people involved in this project?
• Do I expect we will work well together?
• Do they have something special to contribute?
• Are our skills complementary or supplementary?

• Can other people I've met better handle these jobs?
• If I know someone isn't "right" for a project am I willing to move him or her off the project?
• Do I have an agent that can help me secure actors?

Blocked Funds
• Am I producing in a country that has blocked funds?
• Is obtaining blocked funds a realistic route to explore? Why?
• Do I have the contacts and money to obtain this service?
• Do I understand how debt equity and blocked funds work?
• Do I know in what countries debt and blocked funds currently exist?
• Do I have a producer's rep and/or corporate finance banker that I can work with?

Split Rights
• Have I identified all the rights in my property?
• Do I know which can and which cannot be separated when sold?
• Have I realistically evaluated the worth of each of these rights?
• Have I identified buyers for them?
• Have I identified those to be pre-sold and those to be held until the project is complete?

Home Video
• Who are the best distributors for my video? Why?
• What elements in my video are particularly attractive to distributors? Why?
• Is my budget appropriate to the genre and the expected revenue potential of my video? Why?
• Do I have a strong cast?
• Does my video meet the expectations of its audience?
• Is there a strong script?
• What's the difference between a *manufacturer, distributor* and *retailer?*

- Why don't I want a *standard distribution contract*?
- What's an advance?
- What's a guarantee?
- What's the difference?
- On what schedule is a production advance paid out?
- How does P&A relate to a home video advance?
- How might a producer's goal, a theatrical distributor's goal, and a video company's goal differ? How does this affect me?
- How can I set the context for the video deal?
- What are the basic contract terms in a home video contract?
- What am I looking for? What kind of a deal do I want?
- What rights am I **specifically not** granting to a particular distributor? Why?
- What are realistic home video revenues? How do I calculate them? Over what period of time will I receive them?
- How do returns affect my income?
- What's the difference between a returns *reserve* and a returns *allowance*?
- What is the retail price?
- How does retail price affect the royalty?
- Is there a best time to release my video?
- In what territories world-wide does my video have the most potential? Why?
- Do I know exactly what delivery materials I must submit before I get paid?
- Are there any conflicting *holdbacks* that will keep me from releasing my video for a period of time?
- Do I have the rights to all the rights contained in my video?
- When do I expect royalty reports and royalty checks?
- When will I know if I should audit the video distributor's books?

Video Sponsorship

• What's more important: getting production funds or a marketing commitment? Why?
• What are sponsors looking for?
• What are the benefits my project can offer a sponsor?
• What can I give to a sponsor?
• What are all the things I might want from a sponsor? How could a sponsor use my video?
• Can I justify and calculate the number of impressions my video will deliver?
• What companies could use my video as a premium? How?
• Do I have contacts with an advertising or product placement agency?
• Why does the value of my project increase to a distributor when I have a sponsor attached?
• What makes my video sponsorable?
• Can I create a different version of my video for a sponsor?
• How can I create a second distribution window after a premium deal window expires?
• Do I have the time to find and conclude a sponsor deal?
• What are some marketing ideas for my video?
• Who are the target audiences? How does the video serve them?
• Are there manufacturers whose products can be included in my video? How can they use my video in their promotions or sales presentations? What's the value to them? What would they be willing to pay or provide?

Summary

• Do I have the energy necessary to make this film or video?
• Am I able to deal with rejection? Is my intent to make this film strong?

• What will sustain me in order to find the answers and carry out the actions associated with these questions?

• **Why do I want to make this film (video)?** (Spend no less than one hour asking yourself this question over and over. Or have someone else sit in front of you and only ask this question. Write down or record the answers no matter how silly or profound they may be at the time. Go back to your list of answers one week later and see if you can find the real answer in your list—one that you can look to in the months to come for strength and inspiration.)

Good luck and much success in your search for financing.

APPENDIX

APPENDIX

FILM DISTRIBUTORS

Film and video distribution is a very transient business. The addresses and phone numbers of these companies may have changed before you've had a chance to call. Some companies merge, change their names, or go out of business altogether. Good luck.

ABC CIRCLE FILMS, 2040 Avenue of the Stars, 5th Floor, Los Angeles, CA 90067, (213) 557-6860

ALIVE, 8271 Melrose Avenue, Los Angeles, CA 90046, (213) 852-1100

ATLANTIC ENTERTAINMENT GROUP, 8255 Sunset Boulevard, Los Angeles, CA 90046-2400, (213) 650-2500

BUENA VISTA/TOUCHSTONE, 500 S. Buena Vista Street, Burbank, CA 91521, (818) 840-1000

CANNON GROUP, INC., 640 San Vicente Boulevard, Los Angeles, CA 90048, (213) 658-2100

CINECOM INTERNATIONAL FILMS, 1250 Broadway, 33rd Floor, New York, NY 10019, (212) 239-8360

CINEPLEX ODEON CORPORATION, 1925 Century Park East, Suite 300, Los Angeles, CA 90067, (213) 553-5307

CINETEL FILMS, INC., 9200 Sunset Boulevard, Suite 1215, Los Angeles, CA 90069, (213) 550-1067

COLUMBIA PICTURES INC., Columbia Plaza, Burbank, CA 91505, (818) 954-6000

CROWN INTERNATIONAL PICTURES, INC., 8701 Wilshire Boulevard, Beverly Hills, CA 90211, (213) 657-6700

DE LAURENTIIS ENTERTAINMENT GROUP, 8670 Wilshire Boulevard, Beverly Hills, CA 90211, (213) 854-7000.
Also: 720 Fifth Avenue, Suite 100, New York, NY 10019, (212) 399-7700

EXPANDED ENTERTAINMENT, 2222 S. Barrington, Los Angeles, CA 90064, (213) 473-6701

FOX INC., 10201 W. Pico Boulevard, Los Angeles, CA 90035, (213) 277-2211
Also: P.O. Box 900, Beverly Hills, CA 90213

HBO PICTURES, 1100 Avenue of the Americas, 10th Floor, New York, NY 10036, (212) 512-1000

HEMDALE FILM CORPORATION, 1118 N. Wetherly Drive, Los Angeles, CA 90069, (213) 550-6894 and (213) 550-6856

INTERNATIONAL FILM MARKETING, 9440 Santa Monica Boulevard, Suite 707, Beverly Hills, CA 90210, (213) 859-3971

ISLAND PICTURES, 9000 Sunset Boulevard, Suite 700, Los Angeles, CA 90069, (213) 276-4500

LORIMAR TELEPICTURES CORPORATION, 10202 W. Washington Boulevard, Culver City, CA 90232-3783, (213) 280-8000

MGM/UA, 10000 W. Washington Boulevard, Culver City, CA 90232, (213) 280-6000

MIRAMAX, 18 E. 48th Street, Suite 1601, New York, NY 10017, (212) 888-2662

NEW CENTURY/VISTA FILM CO., 1875 Century Park East, Suite 200, Los Angeles, CA 90067, (213) 201-0506

NEW LINE CINEMA, 575 Eighth Avenue, 16th Floor, New York, NY 10018, (212) 239-8880
Also: 1116 N. Robertson Boulevard, Suite 808, Los Angeles, CA 90048, (213) 854-5811

NEW WORLD, 1440 S. Sepulveda Boulevard, Los Angeles, CA 90025, (213) 444-8100

ORION PICTURES INTERNATIONAL, and ORION CLASSICS, 711 Fifth Avenue, New York, NY 10022, (212) 758-5100
Also: 9 W. 57th Street, New York, NY 10019, (212) 980-1117
Also: 1888 Century Park East, Los Angeles, CA 90067, (213) 282-0550

PARAMOUNT PICTURES CORPORATION, 5555 Melrose Avenue, Los Angeles, CA 90038-3197, (213) 468-5000
Also: 1 Gulf & Western Plaza, New York, NY 1002, (212) 333-4600

ROSEBUD RELEASING CORP., 8670 Wilshire Boulevard, Beverly Hills, CA 90211, (213) 652-8459

SAMUEL GOLDWYN COMPANY, 10203 Santa Monica Boulevard, Suite 500, Los Angeles, CA 90067-6403, (213) 552-2255

SKOURAS INTERNATIONAL, 1040 N. Las Palmas, Hollywood, CA 90038, (213) 467-3000

TMS PICTURES, INC., 11111 Santa Monica Boulevard, Suite 1850, Los Angeles, CA 90025, (213) 478-4230

TRANS WORLD ENTERTAINMENT, 6464 Sunset Boulevard, Suite 1100, Hollywood, CA 90028, (213) 461-0467

TRI STAR PICTURES, 1875 Century Park East, 7th Floor, Los Angeles, CA 90067, (213) 201-2300
Also: 711 Fifth Avenue, 12th Floor, New York, NY 10022, (212) 758-3900

UNITED ARTISTS PICTURES, INC., 450 N. Roxbury Drive, Beverly Hills, CA 90210, (213) 281-4000

UNIVERSAL PICTURES, 100 Universal City Plaza, Universal City, CA 91608, (818) 777-1000
Also: 445 Park Avenue, New York, NY 10022, (212) 759-7500

WARNER BROS., 4000 Warner Boulevard, Burbank, CA 91522, (818) 954-6000

VIDEO MANUFACTURERS/SUPPLIERS

ABC VIDEO ENTERPRISES, 2040 Avenue of the Stars, Los Angeles, CA 90067, (213) 557-6600

ACADEMY HOME ENTERTAINMENT, 1 Pine Haven Shore Road, Shelburne, VT 05482, (800) 972-0001

ACTIVE HOME VIDEO, 9300 W. Pico Boulevard, Los Angeles, CA 90035, (800) 824-6109

ADLER VIDEO MARKETING INC., Old Dominion Drive, #360, McLean, VA 22101, (703) 556-8880

AIMS MEDIA, 6901 Woodley Avenue, Van Nuys, CA 91406, (818) 785-4111 or (800) 367-2467

A. I. P. DISTRIBUTION INC., 10726 McCune Avenue, Los Angeles, CA 90034, (213) 559-8835

ARTHUR CANTOR FILMS, 2112 Broadway, Suite 400, New York, NY 10023, (212) 496-5710

AMERICAN HOME VIDEO LIBRARY, 500 Broadway, Suite 1807, New York, NY 10136, (212) 869-2616

AMERICAN MEDIA INC, 1454 30th Street, W. DesMoines, IA, 50265 (800-262-2557.

BARR FILMS, 12801 Schabarum Avenue, P.O. Box 7878, Irwindale, CA

BEACON FILMS INC., 21601 Devonshire Street, Evanston, IL 60202

BEST FILM AND VIDEO CORP., 20501 Ventura Blvd., #255, Woodland Hills, CA 91364, (818) 999-2244 also 98 Cutter Mill Road, Great Neck, NY 11021, (516) 487-4515

BFA EDUCATIONAL MEDIA, 468 Park Avenue South, New York, NY 10016, (212) 684-5910

BLACKHAWK FILMS, 595 Triumph Street, Commerce, CA 90040, (319) 323-

268

8637

BOOK OF THE MONTH CLUB, INC., 485 Lexington Avenue, New York, NY 10017, (212) 867-4300

BOOKSHELF VIDEO, 301-B W. Dyer Road, Santa Ana, CA 92702, (714) 957-0206

BUDGET VIDEO, 540 N. Highland Avenue, Los Angeles, CA 90028, (213) 466-2431

BULLDOG FILMS, Oley, PA 19547, (212) 779-8226

CALLY CURTIS CO., (213) 467-1101

CAPITAL CITY/ABC VIDEO ENTERPRISES, 1825 7th Avenue, New York, NY 10019, (212) 887-6655

CBS VIDEO CLUBS/CBS VIDEO LIBRARY, 1400 N. Fruitridge Avenue, Terre Haute, IN 47811
Also: 1211 Avenue of the Americas, New York, NY 10036, (212) 975-4875

CELEBRITY HOME ENTERTAINMENT, 6320 Canoga Avenue, Penthouse Suite, Woodland Hills, CA 91367, (818) 715-1980

CHRONICLE VIDEO CASSETTES, 4628 Fawn Hill Way, Antioch, CA 94509, (213) 858-0141

CHURCHILL FILMS, 622 N. Robertson Boulevard, Los Angeles, CA 90069, (213) 657-5110

CINEMA GUILD, 1697 Broadway, Suite 802, New York, NY 10019, (212) 246-5522

CINERGY ENTERTAINMENT, 858 12th Street, Suite 8, Santa Monica, CA 90403, (213) 451-2513

COLISEUM VIDEO, 430 W. 54th Street, New York, NY 10019, (212) 489-8156

CORINTH VIDEO, 34 Gansevourt Street, New York, NY 10014, (212) 463-0305

CORONET/MTI, A Division of Simon and Schuster, 108 Wilmot Road, Deerfield, IL 60015, (312) 940-1260 or (800) 621-2131

COVENANT VIDEO, 3200 W. Foster Avenue, Chicago, IL 60625, (800) 621-1290

CRITIC'S CHOICE VIDEO INC., 1020 31st Street, Suite 130, Downer's Grove, IL 60515-5503, (312) 969-8895

CROWN VIDEO, 225 Park Street, New York, NY 10003, (212) 254-1600

CRM FILMS, Carlsbad, CA, (800) 421-0833, (619) 431-9800

DARTNELL, (800) 621-5463.

DIRECT CINEMA LIMITED, Box 69589, Los Angeles, CA 90069, (213) 656-4700

DISCOUNT VIDEO TAPES, 3711 Clark Avenue, Suite B, Burbank, CA 91521, (818) 843-3366

DISNEY HOME VIDEO, 500 S. Buena Vista Street, Burbank, CA 91521, (818) 840-1000

DO-IT-YOURSELF, 12 Euclid Avenue, Charlotte, NC 28203, (704) 342-9608

EMBASSY HOME ENTERTAINMENT, 1901 Avenue of the Stars, Los Angeles, CA 90067, (213) 553-3600

FAITH FOR TODAY, 1100 Rancho Conejo Boulevard, Newbury Park, CA 91320, (805) 499-4363

FAMILY HOME ENTERTAINMENT, 1800 Burbank Boulevard, Woodland Hills, CA 91365, (800) 423-7455

FANLIGHT PRODUCTIONS, 47 Halifax Street, Boston, MA 02130, (617) 524-0980

FILMS FOR THE HUMANITIES, INC., P.O. Box 2053, Princeton, NJ 08543, (609) 452-1128

FIRST RUN VIDEO, 3620 Overland Avenue, Los Angeles, CA 90034, (213) 838-2111

FORUM HOME VIDEO INC, 2400 Broadway Avenue, Suite 100, Santa Monica, CA 90404, (213) 315-7800

FRIES HOME VIDEO, 6922 Hollywood Blvd., Los Angeles, CA 90028, (213) 466-2266

GREENLEAF VIDEO INC., 3230 Nebraska Avenue, Santa Monica, CA 90404, (213) 829-7675

HANNA-BARBERA HOME VIDEO, 3400 Cahuenga Blvd., West Hollywood, CA 90068, (213) 969-1246

HARMONY VISION, 16 N. Robertson Boulevard, Suite 701, Los Angeles, CA 90046, (213) 652-8844

HBO VIDEO INC., 1370 Avenue of the Americas, New York, NY 10019, (212) 977-8990

HI-TOPS, 5730 Buckingham Parkway, Culver City, CA 90230, (213) 216-7900

HOLLYWOOD VIDEO INC., 15951 Arminta Street, Van Nuys, CA 91406, (818) 908-1274

HOME VISION/PMI COMPANY, 5547 N. Ravenswood Avenue, Chicago, IL 60640-1199, (312) 878-2600

INCREASE VIDEO, 8265 Sunset Boulevard, Suite 105, Hollywood, CA 90046, (213) 654-8808

INDEPENDENT UNITED DISTRIBUTORS (IUD), 430 W. 54th Street, New York, NY 10019, (800) 223-0313

INDEPENDENT VIDEO SERVICES, 401 East Tenth Avenue, Suite 160, Eugene, OR 97401

INTERNATIONAL FILM EXCHANGE, 201 West 52nd Street, New York, NY 10019, (212) 582-4318

LIVE ENTERTAINMENT, 15400 Sherman Way, Suite 500, Van Nuys, CA 91406, (800) 908-0303

271

IRS VIDEO, 633 N. La Brea, Los Angeles, CA 90036

JOURNAL FILMS INC., 21601 Devonshire Street, Evanston, IL 60202, (800) 323-5448

J2 COMMUNICATIONS, 10850 Wilshire Boulevard, Suite 1000, Los Angeles, CA 90024, (213) 474-5252

KAROL MEDIA, 22 Riverview Drive, Wayne, NJ 07470, (201) 628-9111

KARTES VIDEO, 10 E. 106th Street, Indianapolis, IN 46280, (317) 844-7403

KID TIME VIDEO, 2340 Sawtelle Boulevard, Los Angeles, CA 90064, (213) 452-9006

KITCHEN, THE, 512 W. 19th Street, New York, NY 10011, (312) 443-3793

KULTUR, 121 Highway 36, West Long Branch, NJ 07764

LASERDISC CORP. OF AMERICA, 2265 East 220th Street, P.O. Box 22782, Long Beach, CA 90801-5782, (213) 835-6177

LAWREN PRODUCTION INC., 21601 Devonshire Street, Evanston, IL 60202, (800) 323-9084

LIBERTY PUBLISHING CO., INC., Suite B-3, 440 South Federal Highway, Deerfield, FL 33441, (305) 360-9000

LIVE ENTERTAINMENT, 15400 Sherman Way, Van Nuys, CA 91410, (818) 778-3230

MALJACK PRODUCTIONS, 15825 Rob Roy Drive, Oak Forest, IL 60452-2799, (800) 323-0442

MASTERVISION, 969 Park Avenue, New York, NY 10028-0322, (212) 879-0448

MCA HOME VIDEO, 100 Universal City Plaza, Universal City, CA 91608-1002, (818) 777-4300

MEDIA HOME ENTERTAINMENT, 5730 Buckingham Parkway, Culver City, CA 90230, (213) 216-7900

MEDICAL ELECTRONIC EDUCATION SERVICE INC., 21601 Devonshire Street, Evanston, IL 60202, (800) 323-9084

MEGEL & ASSOCIATES, 3575 Cahuenga Boulevard West, Suite 249, Los Angeles, CA 90068, (213) 850-3306

MGM/UA HOME VIDEO, 10000 W. Washington Blvd., Culver City, CA 90232-2728

MIRAMAR, 1333 N. Northlake Way, #H, Seattle, WA 98103, (206) 545-4337

MORRIS VIDEO, 730 Monterey Street, #105, Monterey Business Park, Torrance, CA 90503, (213) 533-4800

MTI TELEPROGRAMS, 3710 Commercial Avenue, Northbrook, IL 60062, (800) 323-5343

MYSTIC FIRE VIDEO, P.O. Box 1202, Montauk, NY 11954, (516) 668-1111

NATIONAL AUDIOVISUAL CENTER (GSA), Washington, DC 20409, (301) 763-1881

NATIONAL HEALTH VIDEO INC., 12021 Wilshire Boulevard, Suite 550, Los Angeles, CA 90025, (213) 472-2275

NELSON ENTERTAINMENT, 1901 Avenue of the Stars, Los Angeles, CA 90067, (213) 553-3600

NEW AGE VIDEO INC., P.O. Box 669, Old Chelsea Station, New York, NY 10113, (212) 254-1482

NEW DAY FILMS, 7 Harvard Square, Brookline, MA 02146, (617) 566-5914

NEW WORLD VIDEO, 1888 Century Park East, 5th Floor, Los Angeles, CA 90067, (213) 201-0741

NFL FILMS, 330 Fellowship Road, Mt. Laurel, NJ 08054, (609) 778-1600

NIGHTENGALE-CONANT CORP., 300 N. Lehigh Avenue, Chicago, IL 60648, (800) 572-2770

NORSTAR VIDEO CORP., 1580 Old Bayshore Highway, San Jose, CA 95112,

NOSTALGIA MERCHANT, 6255 Sunset Boulevard, Hollywood, CA 90028, (213) 216-7900

ORION HOME VIDEO, 410 Park Avenue, 7th Floor, New York, NY 10012, (212) 888-4518

PACIFIC ARTS VIDEO, 50 La Cienega Boulevard, Suite 210, Beverly Hills, CA 90211, (213) 657-2233

PARAMOUNT HOME VIDEO, 5555 Melrose Avenue, Hollywood, CA 90038, (213) 956-5000

PBS HOME VIDEO, 50 La Cienega Boulevard, Suite 210, Beverly Hills, CA 90211, (213) 657-2233

PBS VIDEO, 1320 Braddock Place, Alexandria VA 22314, (800) 424-7963

PENNSYLVANIA STATE UNIVERSITY, Audio Visual Services, Specialty Services Bldg., University Park, PA 16801, (814) 865-6314

PERENNIAL EDUCATION INC., 21601 Devonshire Street, Evanston, IL 60202, (800) 323-9089

PHOENIX FILMS/BFA EDUCATIONAL MEDIA, 468 Park Avenue South, New York, NY 10016, (212) 648-5910

PIONEER VIDEO, 200 West Grand Avenue, Montvale, NJ 07645, (201) 573-1122

PRISM ENTERTAINMENT, 1888 Century Park East, Suite 1000, Los Angeles, CA 90067-2501, (213) 277-3270

PROFESSIONAL RESEARCH INC., 21601 Devonshire Street, Evanston, IL 60202, (800) 421-2363

PYRAMID FILM AND VIDEO, Box 1048, Santa Monica, CA 90406, (213) 828-7577

RAEDON ENTERTAINMENT GROUP, 8707-D Lindley Avenue, #173, Northridge, CA, 91325, (818) 349-9862

RANDOM HOUSE HOME VIDEO, 201 E. 50th Street, New York, NY 10022, (212) 872-8030

RCA/COLUMBIA HOME VIDEO, 3500 W. Olive Avenue, 3rd Floor, Burbank, CA 91505, (818) 953-7900

RHINO VIDEO, 2225 Colorado Boulevard, Santa Monica, CA 90404-3721, (213) 828-1980

SALINGER FILMS, (818) 450-1300.

SBI VIDEO, 4901 Forbes Road, Lanham, MD 20706, (301) 459-8000

S. I. VIDEO, 14144 Ventura Blvd., Suite 200, Sherman Oaks, CA 91423, (818) 789-9955

SONY VIDEO, 666 5th Avenue, New York, NY 10103, (212) 445-2275

SOUTH GATE ENTERTAINMENT, 7080 Hollywood Blvd., Suite 307, Hollywood, CA 90028, (213) 962-8530

SPINNAKER SOFTWARE, One Kendall Square, Cambridge, MA 02139, (617) 494-1200

TEACHING FILMS INC., 21601 Devonshire Street, Evanston, IL 60202, (800) 323-9084

TERRA-NOVA FILMS, 9848 S. Winchester Avenue, Chicago, IL 60643, (312) 881-8491

TIME-LIFE VIDEO, 1271 Avenue of the Americas, New York, NY 10020, (212)

552-5940

TODAY HOME ENTERTAINMENT, INC., 9200 Sunset Boulevard, Los Angeles, CA 90069, (213) 278-6490

TOUCHSTONE HOME VIDEO, 500 S. Buena Vista, Burbank, CA 91521, (818) 560-5941

TRAVELNETWORK, P.O. Box 11345, Chicago, IL 60611, (312) 266-9400

TURNER ENTERTAINMENT COMPANY, 6 East 43rd Street, New York, NY 10017, (212) 558-7404

UMBRELLA FILMS, 60 Blake Road, Brookline, MA 02146, (617) 277-6639

UNIVERSITY OF CALIFORNIA, Extension Media Center, 2176 Shattuck Avenue, Berkeley, CA 94704, (415) 642-0460 and 642-5578

USA HOME VIDEO, 7920 Alabama Avenue, Canoga Park, CA 91304, (818) 888-3040

VIDAMERICA, 235 E. 55th Street, New York, NY 10022-4001, (212) 355-1600

VIDEO CASSETTE MARKETING, 37 Eucalyptus Drive, El Segundo, CA 90245

VIDEO DATA BANK, 280 South Columbus Avenue, Chicago, IL 60603, (312) 443-3793

VIDEODISC PUBLISHING INC., 381 Park Avenue South, Suite 1601, New York, NY 10016, (212) 685-5522

VIDEO GEMS, 731 N. La Brea Avenue, Los Angeles, CA 90038, (213) 938-2385 or (800) 421-3252

VIDEO LEARNING RESOURCE GROUP, (215) 896-6600

VIDEO NATURALS, 2590 Glen Green, Suite 6, Los Angeles, CA 90068

VIDEO PUBLISHING HOUSE INC., 10011 E. Touhy Avenue, Suite 580, Des Plaines, IL 60018, (312) 827-1191

VIDEOTAKES, 220 Shrewsbury Avenue, Red Bank, NJ 07701, (201) 747-2444

VIDEOTAPE CATALOG, SMW Video Inc., 803 Russell Boulevard, #2, Davis, CA 95616, (800) 547-0653

VIDEO SCHOOLHOUSE, THE, 167 Central Avenue, Pacific Grove, CA 93950, (408) 375-4474

VIDEO TREASURE INC., 87 Essex Street, Hackensack, NJ 07601, (201) 489-7998

VIDEO YESTERYEAR, P.O. Box C, Sandy Hook, CT 06482, (203) 426-2574

VIRGIN VISION, 6100 Wilshire Blvd., 16th Floor, Los Angeles, CA 90048, (213) 857-5200

VOYAGER COMPANY, THE (laserdiscs), 351 Pacific Coast Highway, Santa Monica, CA 90401, (213) 451-1383

WARNER HOME VIDEO, 4000 Warner Boulevard, Burbank, CA 91522-0001, (818) 954-6000

WOOD KNAPP & COMPANY, 5900 Wilshire Blvd., Los Angeles, CA 90036, (212) 938-2484

XEROX INFORMATION RESOURCES GROUP/PUBLISHING, One Pickwick Plaza, P.O. Box 6710, Greenwich, CT 06836, (203) 625-5675

FOREIGN SALES COMPANIES

These companies sell internationally, sometimes handling all rights foreign and sometimes only theatrical, video, or television. Some handle independent product as well as their own product.

A. B. ENTERPRISES, 1560 Broadway, Suite 1101, New York, NY 10036

ABC DISTRIBUTION CO., 825 Seventh Avenue, New York, NY 10019

ADN ASSOCIATES, LTD., 24A New Quebec Street, London, W1H 7DE England

A.I.P. STUDIOS, 10726 McCune Avenue, Los Angeles, CA 90034

ALLIED VISION LTD., Avon House 360 Oxford Street, London WiN 9HA England

ATLAS INTERNATIONAL FILM GMBH, Burgstrasse 7, D-8000 Munich 2, West Germany

CINEPLEX ODEON FILMS INTERNATIONAL, 1925 Century Park East, Suite 200, Los Angeles, CA 90067

CINETEL FILMS, INC., 3800 W. Alameda Avenue, Suite 825, Burbank, CA 91505

CINAETRUST ENTERTAINMENT CORPORATION, 2121 Avenue of the Stars, 6th Floor, Los Angeles, CA 90067

CORI FILMS INTERNATIONAL, 19 Albermarle Street, Mayfair, London W1, England

CROWN INTERNATIONAL PICTURES, INC., 8701 Wilshire Boulevard, Beverly Hills, CA 90211

CURB/ESQUIRE FILMS, 3907 West Alameda Avenue, Burbank, CA 91505

DAVIAN INTERNATIONAL LIMITED, 144 Boundary Street, 1st Floor, Kowloon, Hong Kong

DISTANT HORIZON LTD., 5-6 Portman Mews South, London W1H 9AU England

EURAMCO INTERNATIONAL/MOBASCO INVESTMENT GROUP, 9430 W. Washington Boulevard, Suite 7, Culver City, CA 90230

FILMS AROUND THE WORLD, 685 Fifth Avenue, Suite 1001, New York, NY 10022

FILMSTAR, INC., 12301 Wilshire Boulevard, Suite 505, Los Angeles, CA 90025

FILMTRUST MOTION PICTURE LICENSING INC., 10490 Santa Monica Boulevard, Los Angeles, CA 90025

FOX/LORBER, 419 Park Avenue South, New York, NY 10016, (212) 686-6777

GAVIN FILM LTD., 120 Wardour Street, London W1V 3LA England

GLINWOOD FILMS LIMITED, Swan House, 52 Poland Street, London W1V 3DF England

GOLDCREST FILMS & TELEVISION, 36-44 Brewer Street, London W1R 3HP England

GOLDEN HARVEST/GOLDEN COMMUNICATIONS, 9884 Santa Monica Boulevard, Beverly Hills, CA 90212-1670

GOLDFARB DISTRIBUTORS, INC., 914 S. Robertson Boulevard, Suite 200, Los Angeles, CA 90035

HEMDALE FILM CORPORATION, 1118 N. Wetherly Drive, Los Angeles, CA 90069

IMAGE ORGANIZATION, 9000 Sunset Boulevard, Suite 915, Los Angeles, CA 90069

INTERCONTINENTAL RELEASING CORPORATION, 10351 Santa Monica Boulevard, Suite 410, Los Angeles, CA 90025

INTERNATIONAL FILM EXCHANGE LTD., 201 West 52nd Street, New York, NY 10019

279

INTER-OCEAN FILM SALES, LTD., 6100 Wilshire Boulevard, Suite 1500, Los Angeles, CA 90048

ITC ENTERTAINMENT GROUP/DISTRIBUTION, 12711 Ventura Boulevard, Suite 440, Studio City, CA 91604

J & M ENTERTAINMENT, 1289 Sunset Plaza Drive, Los Angeles, CA 90069

MANAGEMENT COMPANY ENTERTAINMENT GROUP, 2400 Broadway Avenue, Suite 100, Santa Monica, CA 90404

MANLEY PRODUCTIONS, 111 West 57th Street, Suite 1401, New York, NY 10019

MEDIA HOME ENTERTAINMENT, 5730 Buckingham Parkway, Culver City, CA 90036

MGM/UA, 1111 Santa Monica Boulevard, Suite 524, Los Angeles, CA 90025

MORGAN CREEK INTERNATIONAL, 1875 Century Park East, Suite 200, Los Angeles, CA 90067

NELSON ENTERTAINMENT, 335 North Maple Drive, Suite 350, Beverly Hills, CA 90210

NEW LINE CINEMA, INC., 116 N. Robertson Boulevard, Suite 200, Los Angeles, CA 90048

NEW WORLD INTERNATIONAL/TRANSATLANTIC DISTRIBUTORS, 1440 S. Sepulveda Boulevard, Los Angeles, CA 90025-3458

THE NORKAT COMPANY LTD., 280 S. Beverly Drive, Suite 306, Beverly Hills, CA 90212

NORSTAR ENTERTAINMENT, 86 Bloor Street West, 5th Floor, Toronto, Ontario M5S 1M5 Canada

NORTH AMERICAN RELEASING, 808 Nelson Street, Suite 2204, Vancouver, British Columbia, V62 2H2 Canada

ORION PICTURES INTERNATIONAL, 1888 Century Park East, Los Angeles, CA 90067

OVERSEAS FILM GROUP, 8800 Sunset Boulevard, Suite 302, Los Angeles, CA 90069

PATHE INTERNATIONAL, 8670 Sunset Boulevard, Los Angeles, CA 90069

RANK FILM DISTRIBUTORS, 127 Wardour Street, London W1V 4AD England

SCOTTI BROS. PICTURES, 2114 Pico Boulevard, Santa Monica, CA 90405

SHAPIRO GLICKENHAUS ENTERTAINMENT, 12001 Ventura Place, 4th Floor, Studio City, CA 91604

SILVER STAR FILM CORP., 8833 W. Sunset Boulevard, Suite 406, Los Angeles, CA 90069

SKOURAS PICTURES, INC., 1040 N. Las Palmas Avenue, Bldg. No. 10, Hollywood, CA 90038

SOVEREIGN PICTURES, INC., 11845 W. Olympic Boulevard, Suite 1055, Los Angeles, CA 90064

SUGAR ENTERTAINMENT INC., 15821 Ventura Boulevard, Suite 290, Encino, CA 91436

SALES COMPANY, THE, 62 Shaftesbury Avenue, London W1V 7AA England

SAMUEL GOLDWYN COMPANY, THE, 10203 Santa Monica Boulevard, Suite 500, Los Angeles, CA 90067

TITAN FILM INTERNATIONAL LICENSING, NV, c/o Pueblo Film Churerstrasse 24, CH-8808 Pfaeffikon Switzerland

TRANS WORLD ENTERTAINMENT, 3330 Cahuenga Boulevard West, Suite 500, Los Angeles, CA 90068

VIACOM PICTURES, INC., Showtime, 10 Universal City Plaza, Universal City, CA 91608

VIDMARK ENTERTAINMENT, 2901 Ocean Park Boulevard, Suite 123, Santa Monica, CA 90405-2906

VISION INTERNATIONAL, 3330 West Cahuenga Boulevard, Suite 500, Los Angeles, CA 90068

21ST CENTURY FILM CORPORATION, 8200 Wilshire Boulevard, Beverly Hills, CA 90211

GRANT SOURCES

GRANTS

For me, grants are very time consuming, and not too fruitful. Some people are very good at obtaining grants and I applaud them. The requirements for a successful grant proposal are quite different from the proposals for commercial films and videos. Grant films need to be academically strong with high social and public values. There needs to be a powerful creative team with first-class credentials behind not only the development and writing but also the production.

As corporations have agendas for sponsoring media, so do foundations. Successful presenters are aware of foundation and granting organizations agendas and biases and are able to design their proposals accordingly. This special knowledge gives them an edge when applying for grants. If you are going after corporate sponsorship money, then you'll need to find out what their agenda or charter is before applying. You'll also want to meet them, and find out what they are really about (beyond what it says in the grant application and foundation books) before writing your proposal. To do anything less is really a waste of your time.

Find out how and why the foundation or endowment was created and by whom. What is it's charter? What have they funded in the past? Try to get your hands on some recent applications that were successfully funded through the producers. Finding someone who could introduce you directly to the officers of the foundation is much better than going in cold. Are there people on your team that are known to these officers? Anything you can do to stack the deck in your favor is highly suggested. After all, getting grants is highly competitive and these are the kinds of things your competitors are already doing. If you want to be in the running you're going to have to amass your arsenal of resources and clout.

The good news about grant money is that it has fewer strings attached than does investor money; you rarely have to repay it. As long as you make your film, everyone is happy. It doesn't even have to find wide-spread distribution.

Grants are best suited to non-commercial projects that have no chance of being funded in any other manner. For the most part, these will be educational films and videos and PBS-type television programs.

There are many foundations, endowments and state grant councils to pursue that give funds to non-profit foundations. You may need to find a non-profit fiscal agent to administer the grant monies. The Film Arts Foundation (San Francisco), Independent Documentary Association (Los Angeles), Association of Independent Film and Video (New York), or other such organizations can serve as an "umbrella" and will forward the monies to you. They will charge a small administration fee (about 3 to 5 percent) for doing so. Be sure to check with the fiscal agent to ascertain the holder of the copyright in the program. If the producer holds it, the IRS may claim that the grant money is income to the individual and charge the producer personal income tax on the grant received. If the fiscal agent holds the copyright then the producer is not liable for taxation. Check with a lawyer as well.

There are some high profile grants given in the film and video world. The Independent Feature Project (IFP) is run by independent producers and will be enormously useful in all areas of film production and grant application.

- The National Endowment for the Arts gives up to $25,000

for features and $50,000 for organizations.

• The American Film Institute Independent Filmmaker Program grants up to $20,000 per filmmaker.

• American Playhouse (Corporation for Public Broadcasting) will finance up to $600,000 for a U.S.-produced film on American themes. They will expect that the balance of your budget is already in place. Sometimes your film may play theatrically or on cable before it appears on American Playhouse (PBS). They will receive a profit participation in your project and four plays in three years on PBS (during which time you must keep it off pay, network and basic television networks). They will try to get it to show first on PBS, but this would ruin any chance for a theatrical and/or pay television windows. Therefore, you should try to work out an agreement where your film could be exhibited theatrically before going to PBS. There are many productions that have been successful that have retained the rights to go theatrical and pay television before PBS such as SMOOTH TALK, TESTAMENT, EL NORTE and LONG TIME COMPANION. Home video can sometimes be negotiated to come before the PBS window.

• The NEH (National Endowment for the Humanities), for example, allows the films it funds to earn profits. They expect to share in the profits of films that earn back $50,000 per year, in proportion to their share of the overall funding. Fair enough.

• ITVS (Independent Television Service) has just begun to fund projects in the $10,000 to 300,000 range.

• CPB (Corporation for Public Broadcasting) will not fund programs that are commercial so the grant is a boon for producers with strong dramas or high content programs.

Some projects need funding from both grants and investments. This is particularly problematic for legal and tax reasons. You should consult your lawyer about combining grants and investments. It has been done by filmmakers who've received CPB, American Playhouse, AFI and other grants. NORTHERN LIGHTS was originally funded through a state agency grant and then played commercial theaters. Filmmakers need to be creative. The more financial resources that can be tapped for a production, the better. This simply requires some forethought. Sometimes a grant can be used for production and investment for distribution or vice versa.

Most films made on a grant are not going to return income because they are not conceived as commercial ventures. Without grants most of these films would never be produced.

Some of the non-profit organizations that act as conduits for the grants will want their fee extended into profit-sharing if the film makes money. This is negotiable. Sometimes you can arrange a ceiling on the amount of money that they make from net profits. Discuss this and other aspects of grant-receiving with your accountant because of the tax consequences on how you set up your deal with a non-profit conduit.

A list of foundations and institutions that give film and video grants follows.

FOUNDATIONS

These foundations provide grants for independent film and video production:

AMERICAN FILM INSTITUTE INDEPENDENT FILMMAKER PROGRAM, 2021 North Western Avenue, Los Angeles, CA 90027

CALIFORNIA ARTS COUNCIL, Organization Grants Program, Media Program, 1901 Broadway, Suite A, Sacramento, CA 95818, (916) 445-1530

CALIFORNIA COUNCIL FOR THE HUMANITIES, 312 Sutter Street, Suite 601, San Francisco, CA 91408, (415) 391-1474

CORPORATION FOR PUBLIC BROADCASTING (CPB), Open Solicitation,

Television Program Fund, 1111 16th St., NW, Washington DC, 20036, (202) 293-6160

NATIONAL ENDOWMENT FOR THE ARTS, Film/Video Production, 110 Pennsylvania Avenue, N.W., Washington, DC 20508, (202) 882-5452

WESTERN STATES REGIONAL MEDIA ARTS FELLOWSHIPS, Rocky Mountain Film Center, Hunter 102, Box 316, 18th Street and Colorado Avenue, Boulder, CO 80309-0316, (303) 492-1531

GRANT CONDUITS

BARBARA ARONOISKY LATHAM MEMORIAL AWARDS, The School of the Art Institute of Chicago, Columbus Drive and Jackson Boulevard, Chicago, IL 60803, (312) 443-3937

BENTON FOUNDATION, THE, 1776 K. Street, N.W., Suite 900, Washington, D.C. 20006, (202) 429-7350

BLACK AMERICAN CINEMA SOCIETY, Black Filmmakers Grants Program, 3617 Mont Clair Street, Los Angeles, CA, (213) 737-3292

COLUMBIA FOUNDATION, 1090 Sansome Street, San Francisco, CA 94111, (415) 986-5179

FILM ARTS FOUNDATION, Film Arts Foundation Grants Program, 346 Ninth Street, 2nd Floor, San Francisco, CA 94103

FIVF – FOUNDATION FOR INDEPENDENT VIDEO AND FILM INC., Donor Advised Film and Video Fund, 625 Broadway, 9th Floor, New York, NY 10012

FUNDING EXCHANGE, THE, Paul Robeson Fund for Film and Video, 666 Broadway, New York, NY 10012, (212) 260-8500

INDEPENDENT TELEVISION SERVICE, THE, P.O. Box 65797, Saint Paul, MN 55165

INTER-ARTS OF MARIN AWARDS FOR SMALL PROJECTS, THE, 1000 Sir Francis Drake Boulevard, San Anselmo, CA 94960, (415) 457-9744

JOHN D. AND CATHERINE T MACARTHUR FOUNDATION, THE, 140 South Dearborn Street, Chicago, IL 60603, (312) 726-8000

JOHN GUGGENHEIM MEMORIAL FOUNDATION, 90 Park Avenue, New York, NY 10016, (212) 687-4470

L. J. AND MARY SKAGGS FOUNDATION EFFECT OF MASS MEDIA ON HUMAN BEHAVIOR AND DECISION MAKING, 1221 Broadway, 21st Floor, Oakland, CA 94612, (415) 451-3300

LONG BEACH MUSEUM OF ART ARTISTS AWARD ACCESS, 2300 East Ocean Boulevard, Long Beach, CA 90803, (213) 439-2119

LONG BEACH MUSEUM OF ART, Open Channels: Television Production Grant Program, 2300 East Ocean Boulevard, Long Beach, CA 90803, (213) 439-2119

LOS ANGELES CONTEMPORARY EXHIBITIONS INTERDISCIPLINARY GRANTS PROGRAM, 31 Prince Street, Rochester, NY 14607, (716) 442-8676

PIONEER FUND, THE, Box 33, Inverness, CA 94937, (415) 669-1122

RETIREMENT RESEARCH FOUNDATION NATIONAL MEDIA AWARDS, The Center for New Television, 11 East Hubbard Street, Chicago, IL 60611, (312) 565-1787

SAN FRANCISCO FOUNDATION, James D. Phelan Art Award in Video, 500 Washington Street, 8th Floor, San Francisco, CA 94111, (415) 392-0600

WILLIAM BINGHAM FOUNDATION, THE, 1250 Leader Building, Cleveland, OH 44114, (216) 781-3270

WOMEN IN FILM FOUNDATION COMPLETION GRANTS, 6464 Sunset Boulevard, Suite 660, Los Angeles, CA 90028, (213) 463-6040

ZELLERBACH FAMILY FUND COMMUNITY ARTS DISTRIBUTION COMMITTEE, 260 California Street, Suite 1010, San Francisco, CA 94111, (415) 421-2629

ADDITIONAL SOURCES

EDUCATIONAL FILM & TELEVISION CENTER, Fiscal Sponsorship Program, 210 Fifth Avenue, Suite 1102, New York, NY 10010

FORD FOUNDATIONS, THE, Division of Humanities and the Arts, 320 East 43rd Street, New York, NY 10017

JEROME FOUNDATION, THE, St. Paul, MN 55101

JOHN AND MARY MARKLE FOUNDATION, THE, 75 Rockefeller Plaza, Suite 1800, New York, NY 10019

LEARNING CHANNEL, THE, 1525 Wilson Boulevard, Suite 550, Rosslyn, VA 22209

MCA FOUNDATION LTD., 100 Universal City Plaza, Universal City, CA 91608

NATIONAL ENDOWMENT FOR THE ARTS, Grants Office, 2401 E. Street, N.W., Washington, D.C. 20506

SCRIPPS HOWARD FOUNDATION, P.O. Box 5380, Cincinnati, OH 45201

STEP-UP COMPLETION FUND, PBS Programming, 1320 Braddock Place, Alexandria, VA 22314

Worth Contacting

Alcoa Foundation, PA
Andrew W. Mellon Foundation, The
Atlantic Richfield Foundation, CA
ATT Foundation, NY
Bank America Foundation, CA
California Community Foundation
CBS Foundation
CPB: The Revolving Documentary Fund
Disney Foundation, CA
Eastman Kodak Company
General Electric Foundation, CT
General Motors Foundation, MI
Mobil Foundation, NY
NEH Media Program of the Division of Public Programs
NEH Division of Special Program Corp for Public Broadcasting
PBS
RCA Corp.
TRW Foundation
WNET/13, NY

BIBLIOGRAPHY

FINANCING & PRODUCTION

FINANCING YOUR FILM: A GUIDE FOR INDEPENDENT FILMMAKERS AND PRODUCERS by Trisha Curran, Praeger Publishers, 1 Madison Avenue, New York, NY 10010

INDEPENDENT PRODUCER: FILM & TELEVISION, THE, by Hourcourt, Howlett, Davies, Moskovic, Faber & Faber, London (1986)

OFF-HOLLYWOOD: THE MAKING & MARKETING OF INDEPENDENT FILMS by David Rosen with Peter Hamilton, from Grove Weidenfeld, 841 Broadway, New York, NY 10003-4793

PRODUCERS ON PRODUCING: THE MAKING OF FILM & TELEVISION by Irv Broughton, MacFarland Publishing (1986)

DISTRIBUTION

DISTRIBUTION GUIDE BY THE INDEPENDENT FILM JOURNAL, 1251 Avenue of the Americas, New York, NY

DOING IT YOURSELF: A HANDBOOK ON INDEPENDENT FILM DISTRIBUTION by AIVF, Inc. by Julia Reichert, 99 Prince Street, New York, NY 10012 (1977)

ENTERTAINMENT INDUSTRY ECONOMICS by Harold L. Vogel, Cambridge University Press, New York, NY (1986)

FILM INDUSTRIES: PRACTICAL BUSINESS AND LEGAL PROBLEMS IN PRODUCTION, DISTRIBUTION AND EXHIBITION, THE, by Michael F. Mayer, available from Hastings House, New York, NY (1978)—$11.50

INDEPENDENT FILM AND VIDEOMAKERS GUIDE, THE by Michael Wiese, Revised and Expanded 1990, available from Michael Wiese, 3960 Laurel Canyon Boulevard, #331, Studio City, CA 91604—$20.95 postpaid

MAKING FILMS YOUR BUSINESS by Mollie Gregory, available from Schocken Books, New York, NY (1979)—$6.95

292

MOTION PICTURE DISTRIBUTION—BUSINESS OR RACKET? by Walter E. Hurst and Wm. Storm Hale, Seven Arts, Hollywood, CA (1975)

PRODUCING, FINANCING AND DISTRIBUTING FILM by Farber and Baumgarten, Drama Book Specialists, New York, NY (1973)

THE MOVIE BUSINESS: AMERICAN FILM INDUSTRY PRACTICE by William Bluem and Jason Squire, Hastings House, New York (1972)

16MM DISTRIBUTION by Judith Trojan & Nadien Convert, available from Educational Film Library Association, 43 W. 61st Street, New York, NY 10023— $6

VIDEO

ALTERNATIVE VISIONS: DISTRIBUTING INDEPENDENT MEDIA IN A HOME VIDEO WORLD by Debra Franco, available from AIVF, 625 Broadway, 9th Floor, New York, NY 10012

GUIDE TO VIDEOTAPE PUBLISHING, ed. by Ellen Lazer, available from Knowledge Industry Publications, 701 Westchester Avenue, White Plains, NY 10604 (1986)

HOME VIDEO IN LIBRARIES: HOW LIBRARIES BUY AND CIRCULATE PRERECORDED HOME VIDEO, Martha Dewing, Knowledge Industry Publications, White Plaines, NY, 1988

HOME VIDEO: PRODUCING FOR THE HOME MARKET by Michael Wiese, available from Michael Wiese, 3690 Laurel Canyon Boulevard, #331, Studio City, CA 91604—$18.95 postpaid

HOME VIDEO PUBLISHING: THE DISTRIBUTION OF VIDEOCASSETTES 1986-90 by Presentation Consultants Inc. White Plains, NY: Knowledge Industry Publications, Inc., 1986

AN INTRODUCTION TO THE 800# REVOLUTION; DIRECT-TO VIEWER MARKETING OF HOME VIDEO by Peter Hamilton, in NVR Reports (1990). Available from National Video Resources, 73 Spring Street, Suite 606, New York, NY 10012.

THE NEXT STEP by Morrie Warshawski, available from AIVF, 625 Broadway, 9th Floor, New York, NY 10012

VARIETY'S COMPLETE HOME VIDEO DIRECTORY, R.R. Bowker, New York, NY (1988)

VIDEO PRODUCT MARKETPLACE by Martin Porter, Martin Porter & Associates Publications, Port Washington, NY (1987)

VIDEO TAPE & DISC GUIDE TO HOME ENTERTAINMENT, THE, National Video Clearinghouse, Inc., Syosset, NY (annual)

DIRECTORIES

AMERICAN DEMOGRAPHICS, Dow Jones and Company Inc., Syracuse, NY

MOTION PICTURE, TV AND THEATER DIRECTORY, Motion Picture Enterprises, Tarrytown, NY 10591—$4.25

NEW YORK FEATURE FILM AND VIDEO GUIDE, 90 Riverside Drive, New York, NY 10024—$5

PRODUCER'S MASTER GUIDE, THE, New York Production Manual Inc., 611 Broadway, Suite 807, New York, NY 10012—$69.95 per year

TELEVISION AND CABLE CONTACTS, Larimi Communications Associates, Ltd., 5 W. 37th Street, New York, NY 10018, (212) 819-9310

1991 FILM DIRECTORS, 1991 FILM PRODUCERS, STUDIOS AND AGENTS GUIDE, 1991 CINEMATOGRAPHERS, PRODUCTION DESIGNERS, COSTUME DESIGNERS & FILM EDITORS GUIDE by Kate Bales, available from Lone Eagle Publishing, 9903 Santa Monica Boulevard,

Beverly Hills, CA 90212, (213) 471-8066

1991 MOTION PICTURE ALMANAC & TELEVISION ALMANAC (2 books), available from Quigley Publishing Company, 159 W. 53rd Street, New York, NY 10019

GRANTS

ENCYCLOPEDIA OF ASSOCIATIONS by Robert Thomas and Denise Allard, Detroit, MI, Gale Research, 1987, U.S. nonprofit organizations

FOUNDATION CENTER, THE, 79 Fifth Avenue, Dept. KM, New York, NY 10003 will do a computer search ($45 fee) listing the foundations that regularly grant monies to fund film and video projects

FOUNDATION GRANTS TO INDIVIDUALS from The Foundation Center, NY

GET THE MONEY AND SHOOT: THE DRI GUIDE TO FUNDING DOCUMENTARY FILMS by Bruce Jackson and Diane Christian, Buffalo, NY, Documentary Reserach, revised edition 1986

GRANT GUIDES FOR THE ARTS, The Foundation Center, NY

NATIONAL DIRECTORY OF GRANTS AND AID TO INDIVIDUALS IN THE ARTS Washington International Newsletter, Washington, D.C.

SPONSORS: A GUIDE FOR VIDEO AND FILM, American Council for the Arts, New York, NY

SUPPORTING YOURSELF AS AN ARTIST: A PRACTICAL GUIDE by Deborah A. Hoover, American Council for the Arts/Oxford University Press, New York, NY

SPONSORSHIP

GUIDE TO THE SPONSORED VIDEO by Doug Duda, et al., available from Knowledge Industry Publications, 701 Westchester Avenue, White Plains, NY 10604 (1987)

SPONSORSHIP, PRINCIPLES AND PRACTICES by Ron Bergin, Amusement

295

Business, Box 24970, Nashville, TN 37302, (615) 321-4254

TRADE PUBLICATIONS

AD AGE, 200 E. 42nd Street, New York, NY 10017

ADVERTISING AGE, Crain Communications, Inc., 740 N. Rush Street, Chicago, IL 60611

ADWEEK, 49 E. 21st Street, New York, NY 10010

AMERICAN CINEMATOGRAPHER, 220 E. 42nd Street, Suite 930, New York, NY 10017

AMERICAN FILM, The American Film Institute, Washington DC

BACKSTAGE, 5151 Wilshire Boulevard, Suite 302, Los Angeles, CA 90036

BILLBOARD, 9107 Wilshire Boulevard, #2265, Los Angeles, CA 90036. Also: 1515 Broadway, New York, NY 10036

BROADCASTING, 630 Third Street, 12th Floor, New York, NY 10017. *Also:* Broadcasting Publications Inc., Washington, DC

CHAIN STORE AGE, Lebhar-Friedman, Inc., New York, NY

CHANNELS, 19 West 44th Street, #812, New York, NY 10036

CHANNELS OF COMMUNICATION, Media Commentary Council, Inc., New York, NY

CHILDREN'S VIDEO, John L. Weber for Children's Video Magazine, Inc., Brooklyn, NY

COMING ATTRACTIONS, Convenience Video Corp., Jersey City, NJ

CONVENIENCE STORE NEWS, BMT Publications, Inc., New York, NY

DAILY VARIETY, 1400 N. Cahuenga Boulevard, Los Angeles, CA 90028

DEALERSCOPE, North American Publishing Co., Philadelphia, PA

DIRECT MARKETING, Hoke Communications, Inc., Garden City, NY

DM [Direct Marketing] NEWS, c/o DMN Corp., 19 W. 21st Street, New York, NY 10010, (212) 741-2095

ELECTRONIC MEDIA, 220 East 42nd Street, #1306, New York, NY 10017

ELECTRONIC RETAILING, Fairchild Publications, New York, NY

FILM COMMENT, 140 W. 65th Street, New York, NY 10023

FILM JOURNAL, 244 W. 49th Street, #305, New York, NY 10019

FOLIO, Folio Magazine Publishing Corp., New Canaan, CT

HOLLYWOOD REPORTER, 1501 Broadway, New York, NY 10036
Also: 6715 Sunset Boulevard, Hollywood, CA 90028

HOME VIDEO PUBLISHER, Knowledge Industry Publications, 701 Westchester Avenue, White Plains, NY 10604

HOME VIEWER, 11 N. Second Street, Philadelphia, PA 19160, (215) 629-1588

INTV JOURNAL, 80 Fifth Avenue, New York, NY 10011

LIBRARY JOURNAL, R.R. Bowker Co., New York, NY

MART, Morgan-Grampian Publishing Co., New York, NY

MILLIMETER, 826 Broadway, New York, NY 10003

MOVIELINE, 1141 S. Beverly Drive, Los Angeles, CA 90035-1139

MULTI-CHANNEL NEWS, 7 E. 12th Street, New York, NY 10003

NEWS & VIEWS, 1560 Broadway, #714, New York, NY 10036

PAUL KAGAN ASSOCIATES, 126 Clock Tower Place, Carmel, CA 93923

PHOTOMETHODS, Ziff-Davis Publishing Co., New York, NY

PHOTO WEEKLY, Billboard Publications Inc., New York, NY

PREMIERE, 755 Second Avenue, New York, NY 10017

PUBLISHERS WEEKLY, R.R. Bowker Co., New York, NY

ROCKAMERICA MAGAZINE, 27 E. 21st Street, New York, NY 10010

SCREEN INTERNATIONAL, 8500 Wilshire Boulevard, Beverly Hills, CA 90211

SIGHT & SOUND MARKETING, Dorbaugh Publications, New York, NY

SPLICE, 10 Columbus Circle, #1300, New York, NY 10019

TAPE BUSINESS, Knowledge Industry Publications, 701 Westchester Avenue, White Plains, NY 10604

TELEVISION DIGEST, Television Digest Inc., 475 Fifth Avenue, Suite 1021, New York, NY 10017

TV/RADIO AGE, 1270 Avenue of the Americas, #502, New York, NY 10020

TWICE, 5900 Wilshire Boulevard, #700, Los Angeles, CA 90036

V, THE MAIL ORDER MAGAZINE OF VIDEOCASSETTES, Fairfield Publishing Co., Inc., New York, NY

VARIETY (weekly edition, also available as a daily), Variety, Inc., 154 W. 46th Street, New York, NY 10036—$75 per year

VIDEO BUSINESS WEEKLY, 345 Park South, New York, NY 10010

VIDEO INSIDER, 223 Conestoga Road, Wayne, PA 19087

VIDEO MAGAZINE, 460 W. 34th Street, New York, NY 10001, (212) 947-6500

VIDEO MARKETING NEWSLETTER, 12052 Montecito Road, Los Alamitos, CA 90720

VIDEO MARKETPLACE, World Publishing Corp., Evanston, IL

VIDEO PREVIEW, P.O. Box 561467, Dallas, TX 75356-1476, (214) 438-4111

VIDEO REVIEW, 902 Broadway, New York, NY 10010, (212) 477-2200

VIDEO SOFTWARE DEALER, 5519 Centinela Avenue, Los Angeles, CA 90066

VIDEO STORE, 545 Fifth Avenue, New York, NY 10017. *Also:* 1700 E. Dyer Road, Santa Ana, CA 92705

VIDEO STORE (and ENTERTAINMENT MERCHANDISING), Magacycle Inc., Irvine, CA

VIDEO WEEK, 475 Fifth Avenue, New York, NY 10017

VIEW MAGAZINE, 80 Fifth Avenue, #501, New York, NY

VIEW: THE MAGAZINE OF CABLE TV PROGRAMMING, Subscription Services Department, P.O. Box 5011, FDR Station, New York, NY 10022—$36 per year

AVAILABLE FROM

MICHAEL

WIESE

PRODUCTIONS

SUCCESSFUL FINANCING AND DISTRIBUTION

FILM & VIDEO MARKETING
by Michael Wiese

1989, 512 pages, 77 illustrations
ISBN 0-941188-05-1, $18.95

"Marketing" is an oft-heard catch word of the '90's,
but few producers understand the hidden value
marketing brings to the success of their films and
videos. In the highly competitive film and video
markets, conceiving an idea worthy of production is only half the battle. This
insider's book shares industry techniques one can use to sell investors, exhibitors,
distributors, home video suppliers, wholesalers, retailers and the buying public.

A comprehensive guide to film and video marketing and distribution techniques
for low budget features and home video programs. Includes developing hit ideas,
selling the buyer, market research, getting to your audience, getting distributors,
marketing and promotion, packaging and key art, publicity and advertising,
specialized markets, release strategies, and a marketing case study of DIRTY
DANCING.

INDEPENDENT FILM & VIDEOMAKERS GUIDE
by Michael Wiese

Revised Edition 1990, 392 pages, 45 illustrations
ISBN 0-941188-02-7, $18.95

A classic best-seller and independent producer's best
friend. Advice on limited partnerships, writing a
prospectus, market research, negotiating, film markets,
pay TV and home video buyers.

Contents include:

- Financing
- Finding Distributors
- Investor Presentations
- Income Projectsion
- Partnership Agreements
- Promotion

*"This book is full of practical tips on how to get a film or video project financed, produced,
and distributed without sacrificing artistic integrity."*
CO-EVOLUTION QUARTERLY

FILM & VIDEO BUDGETS
By Michael Wiese

Revised 1988, 348 pages, 18 budgets
ISBN 0-941188-02-7, $16.95

This is a basic "how-to" budget guide for many types of films. Clearly written, informal in style, and generously illustrated with detailed budgets. Readers can look up sample budgets similar to their own and find a wealth of information on costs and savings.

Includes:
- Money-Saving Tips
- Computer Budgets
- Line Items
- Accounting Procedures
- Negotiations
- Union /Guild Contacts

"...must reading. This is a common-sense book written with a touch of ironic humor. If you want to make your life easier in the financial arena of film/video making—buy the book. Enjoyable reading for those who like profits." INFO. FILM PRODUCERS ASSOC.

HOME VIDEO:
Producing for the Home Market

By Michael Wiese

1986, 370 pages, 56 illustrations,
ISBN 0-941188-04-3, $16.95

A clear, comprehensive book that brings together advice on the successful development and distribution of original home video programs. Genres such as comedy, how-to, documentaries, children's, sponsored and music videos are discussed in detail. The book examines new marketing opportunities for independent producers.

- Creative Ideas
- Marketing
- Video Budgets
- Pitching Projects
- Program Genres
- Tips on Contracts
- Financing and Co-Productions
- Finding Distributors
- Secrets of Packaging

"The reader is bombarded with timely information on virtually all phases of marketing to the home video audience. Might be the single most valuable book a videomaker can read. A cannot-do-without book for the shelf of any video producer. " VIDEOMAKER

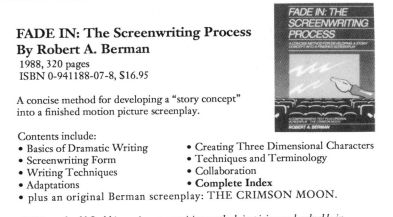

FADE IN: The Screenwriting Process
By Robert A. Berman
1988, 320 pages
ISBN 0-941188-07-8, $16.95

A concise method for developing a "story concept"
into a finished motion picture screenplay.

Contents include:
- Basics of Dramatic Writing
- Screenwriting Form
- Writing Techniques
- Adaptations
- Creating Three Dimensional Characters
- Techniques and Terminology
- Collaboration
- **Complete Index**
- plus an original Berman screenplay: THE CRIMSON MOON.

*"Writers should find his concise screenwriting methods inspiring and valuable in
enhancing their own creative skills. "*   MICHAEL WIESE

FILM DIRECTING SHOT BY SHOT
by Steven D. Katz
376 pages, 7 x 10, 1991, 750 illustrations, storyboards
& photographs
ISBN 0-941188-10-8, $24.95

A complete catalogue of visual techniques and their
stylistic implication for both the filmmaker and
videomaker—a "textbook" which enables working
filmmakers (as well as screenwriters and others) to
expand their stylistic knowledge.

Contents include:
- Visualization Tools
- Staging Dialogue Scenes
- Framing/Composition
- Storyboard Style
- Camera Techniques
- Blocking Shots
- Continuity Style
- Camera Movement
- Script Analysis

Over 750 illustrations and photographs plus original storyboards from Spielberg's
EMPIRE OF THE SUN, Hitchcock's THE BIRDS, and Welles' CITIZEN
KANE.

An essential book for both seasoned and novice filmmakers.

305

AUDIO TAPE

The American Film Institute

presents

FINANCING & PRODUCING VIDEO
Winning Strategies for Creative Producers

A One-Day Seminar with Michael Wiese

An edited audiotape (approximately 4 hours) of this comprehensive one-day seminar by Michael Wiese covers program development, co-productions, financing structures, pitching, distribution deals, sponsorship, creative marketing and a variety of insider's financing and marketing strategies for successful video productions.

"The next best thing to being there.'

ISBN 0-941188-12-4, $49.95, Approximately 4 hours.

If MAD, SPY and NATIONAL LAMPOON ever got together....

THE HOLLYWOOD GIFT CATALOG

**Written and Illustrated
by Ernie Fosselius ("HARDWARE WARS")**

48 hilarious pages, 100 outrageous illustrations, ISBN 0-941188-06-X, $2.95
Special "Wrap Party Special"—10 books/$19.95

HOLLYWOOD GIFT CATALOG is a catalog parody which contains over 100 items that might be found on the desks of Hollywood's Great and Near-Great.

Don't hand these out before a shoot—your crew will never get any work done!

ORDER FORM

MICHAEL WIESE PRODUCTIONS
3960 Laurel Canyon Blvd., Suite 331,
Studio City, CA 91604-3791

Please send the following:

Quantity

	Price	Sub-Total
____ FILM AND VIDEO MARKETING	$ 18.95	= _____
____ INDEPENDENT FILM AND VIDEOMAKERS GUIDE	18.95	= _____
____ FILM AND VIDEO BUDGETS	18.95	= _____
____ HOME VIDEO: Producing for the Home Market	16.95	= _____
____ FADE IN: The Screenwriting Process	16.95	= _____
____ HOLLYWOOD GIFT CATALOG	2.95	= _____
____ "Wrap Party Special" (10 Hollywood Gift Catalogs)	19.95	= _____
____ FILM DIRECTING SHOT BY SHOT	24.95	= _____
____ FILM & VIDEO FINANCING	22.95	= _____
____ FINANCING & PRODUCING VIDEO (Audiotape)	49.95	= _____

SUBTOTAL _____
DISCOUNT - _____
SHIPPING/HANDLING (See below) + _____
Calif. RESIDENTS add 6.5% SALES TAX + _____

TOTAL : $_____

Enclosed is $_____. Check or money order payable to *Michael Wiese Productions.*

Name:_____

Address:

City:_____ State: _____ Zip:_____

Telephone: (__) _____

Allow 2-3 weeks for delivery.   FVF

SHIPPING & HANDLING:

   1 book $2.00
   2 books 3.50
   3 books 4.00
   Each book thereafter 1.00

ALL NON–USA ORDERS
Must be Prepaid:
Add $4.00 each via surface mail.
Add $7.00 each via air mail.

DISCOUNTS:
20% 4 copies or more
30% 6 copies or more
40% 15 copies or more
44% 25 copies or more

(All prices subject to change without notice.)

CONSULTING SERVICES

MICHAEL WIESE PRODUCTIONS offers a consulting service to producers, directors, writers, media creators, distributors, suppliers, publishers and others to provide expert advice and strategies for film and home video.

MWP works with a limited number of consulting clients at any one time. Only those clients where MWP feels that a real value will be added to their endeavors will be selected.

Both large and small clients may be considered. Rates include a one-time, initial consultation rate or an on-going monthly retainer.

Clients include:

NATIONAL GEOGRAPHIC
THE SMITHSONIAN INSTITUTION
BUCKMINSTER FULLER INSTITUTE
THE AMERICAN FILM INSTITUTE
MYSTIC FIRE VIDEO
PACIFIC ARTS VIDEO
PBS HOME VIDEO
NAUTILUS–JAPAN
WNET-PBS-NEW YORK
KTEH-PBS-SAN JOSE
KCET-PBS– LOS ANGELES
THE APOLLO THEATER PRODUCTIONS

Consulting areas include program development, financing structure, budgeting, licensing, production, marketing strategy, sales, promotion, outreach, release planning, fulfillment, sponsorship and more.

For information or an appointment call (818) 905-6367 or fax (818) 986-3408.